sheer style

sheer style

TESSA EVELEGH

LAUREL
GLEN

To Richard, Zoë and Faye

First published in the United States in 2000 by
Laurel Glen Publishing
An imprint of the Advantage Publishers Group
5880 Oberlin Drive, San Diego, CA 92121-4794
www.advantagebooksonline.com

Published in Great Britain in 2000 by Collins & Brown Ltd, London House,
Great Eastern Wharf, Parkgate Road, London SW11 4NQ

ISBN 1-57145-653-8

Library of Congress Cataloging-in-Publication Data available upon request.

A BERRY BOOK
Conceived, edited, and designed by Susan Berry for Collins & Brown
Designer: Debbie Mole
Illustrator: Kate Simunek
Editor: Corinne Asghar

North American Edition
Publisher: Allen Orso
Managing Editor: JoAnn Padgett
Project Editor: Elizabeth McNulty

1 2 3 4 5   00 01 02 03 04 05

Reproduction by Classic Scan, Singapore

Printed and bound in Hong Kong

Contents

Sheer fascination

Light filtering through sheer fabrics and playing upon their surface gives them a diaphanous beauty. Their translucence creates an entrancing air of mystery that simply adds to their allure.

SIMPLE ORGANDY PANELS billowing at the French doors that open into our garden still lift my spirits every time I pass them. Ever since I hung them several years ago, wondering if they really were the sensible choice for a spot where muddy feet pass in and out, I've been fascinated by the effect that they've had on the light in the room. It isn't simply that sheer panels block off less light than traditional drapes: they seem to reflect extra light around the room. Scientific explanations are beyond me, but certain sheers undoubtedly have a reflective quality. When we hung a diaphanous burgundy dress behind a pure white cotton organdy panel at the window (see page 8), its shadow reflected back off the curtain giving a curious double image. Perhaps the ambient light bounces off the white organdy panel and around our dining room in the same way. Happily, since I bought those first panels, the choice of sheer fabrics has grown enormously and many fabric designers have promoted them in their collections. Traditionally, sheer fabrics were used primarily for privacy, rather than for their own beauty. But sheers are no longer an afterthought in interior design. From my point of view, this is a welcome trend. Enthusiasm for sheers and natural

Left *Sheer fabrics are not reserved for window treatments. Draped over a bed, a delicate cotton voile creates a romantic atmosphere without obscuring the light. The translucency of fine fabrics means that you can see layer through layer, which creates a sense of depth. It also means that colors can mix or become richer, just as paint colors can be mixed and intensified on an artist's palette. That effect is demonstrated here by the difference in shade when the voile is seen as a single thickness and when it is seen as three thicknesses, which makes the colors appear more intense. In this way you can create a wealth of shades.*

Right *The light-reflective properties of white cotton organdy are closely illustrated here. The sun streaming in through the window behind casts a shadow of the dress onto the back of the organdy and back onto the window, creating an intriguing double reflection.*

Opposite (top) *While translucency allows you to see through to another area, it also adds a sense of mystery by veiling the view. Here, the flowers and soaps behind an organdy curtain take on an air of romance when partially obscured from view by the ethereal fabric.*

Opposite (bottom) *The gossamer quality of sheers has a glorious effect on their colors. This metallic organza is lilac shot with aqua, yet the translucency of the fabric allows the colors to mix visually like watercolor paints. These fabrics invite you to experiment with color and texture to create an individual look.*

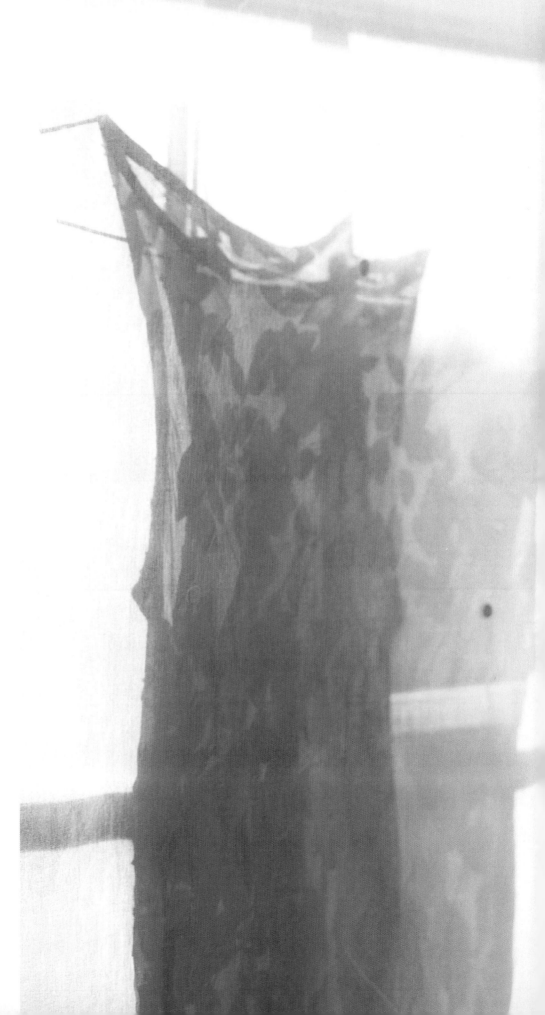

only be touched upon in a book of this size. As well as sheer fabric, there is a vast array of other materials, such as pierced metals, laminates, tracing paper, even plastic wrap, that can be used for translucent effect. This book offers just a taste of what I think will be an increasing enthusiasm for all things translucent in and around the home. As well as looking at light, translucency, and veiling, it deals with practical considerations that are particular to working with sheer materials. I hope the projects will provide you with inspiration. You can follow them step by step if you like or simply use them to help you think of your own ideas for living with light.

daylight can take you beyond the windows into the rest of the home, extending the effect of natural daylight into every part of the house. A translucent screen or room divider creates zones within a larger space, yet allows light through from one area to another, thus retaining the airy feel of open-plan living.

It is easy to become captivated by the effect created by sheer materials. As well as enhancing the natural light within an interior, they can also be used as veils. Any translucent fabric can evoke a fascination with what lies beyond—a soft, billowing sheer curtain could be screening a tantalizingly beautiful scene that can only be glimpsed when the wind blows the fabric. Alternatively, a sheer blind could be used to mask a less-than-perfect view and reduce the harsh reality of the outside world.

The wealth of translucent materials and their myriad uses can

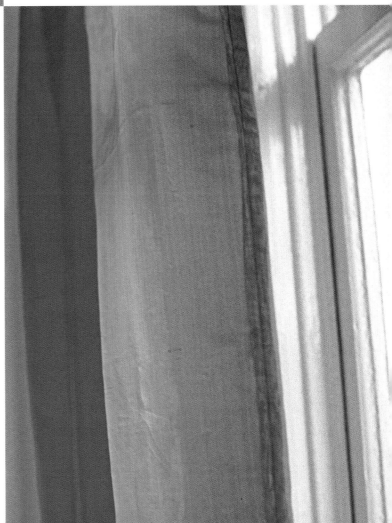

Architectural use of light

The traditional use of heavy drapes is increasingly being replaced by a demand for window treatments that allow more natural light indoors. Daylight-filled atriums, shopping malls, and office buildings are inspiring people to create lighter, brighter homes.

Rooms that are bathed in natural light evoke in us a deep-seated sense of well-being. The subtle play of light and shadow as the day progresses from dawn to twilight provides a feeling of peace and contentment. Deprived of light, we suffer both physically and emotionally. Many people living in northern latitudes know only too well the effects of aptly-named SAD, (seasonal affective disorder) a recognized form of depression typically suffered in the dark winter months. Responding to this need for natural light, architects through the ages have sought to build houses that focus on optimum levels of natural light. In sunny countries, this involves cutting down on midday glare using verandas, shutters, and screens as buffers. However, in northern climes, the quest is to bring in as much light as possible. Scandinavian homes are famed for their large windows, uncluttered spaces,

Left & opposite Glass doors with windows above bring new light to an old building. A series of Roman blinds control the amount of light entering the room.

painted furniture, and pastel color schemes, all of which help to encourage as much natural light as possible into and around the home.

On the other hand, some northern countries have been distracted by the advent of electric light. At the beginning of the twentieth century, this was seen as a magical solution to the perennial problem of balancing the need for heat conservation with the need for light. Living in a chilly climate, people favored thick heavy drapes. Curtains were drawn against the winter cold and electric lights were used in place of natural illumination. But the last few years have seen major change. Central heating makes the house feel cozy and architects can return to introducing as much light as possible to their buildings. Electric light inside the house is 100 times less powerful than the light outside on a cloudy day and 1,000 times less than daylight on a sunny day.

Overhead light is considerably brighter than that which enters a building horizontally though the window. Traditionally, the solution has been to use skylights to bring daylight directly into the gloomier parts of buildings. Now, new technology has enabled architects to build buildings with a far greater degree of translucency. Daylight streams through plate-glass walls, glass bricks, and multistory atriums in apartments, office buildings, and shopping malls, allowing in up to ten times more light than usual. Inured to this level of light this during the day, we are demanding more light and translucency in our homes. At the same time, we are surrounded by more and more translucent objects in everyday life. Daily, we gaze at television and computer screens whose images seem to dance through glass; you can even buy translucent computers and game consoles. Packaging, book bindings, watches, and even vacuum cleaners have taken on a translucent appearance. The fashion industry, too, is bringing translucent, if not transparent, clothes onto the catwalk.

Left *This modern extension has three skylights, allowing plenty of good-quality light into the room.*

Center *Windows at two levels, plus a corner window, allow for several aspects of incoming light, flooding the room with light.*

We are, perhaps, on the cusp of change. Light and lightness, along with translucency and luminescence, have become key concepts for a significant number of architects and designers.

It is not such a large leap from corporate buildings to our own home surroundings, and the future looks bright, in more ways than one. However, we must remember that our world does not wholly consist of new, light-filled buildings—nor would we want it to. While it is obviously not desirable to get rid of all old buildings, we can adapt these buildings to bring more light into them. Sky-lights, dormer windows, glass-roofed room extensions, and even glass-brick walls can all make a vast difference in the way a building looks from inside. Take a tip from interior designers and use gossamer, light-reflective sheers and a wealth of other translucent materials in your own home to mimic the trend toward all things light and beautiful.

Right *This glass-block wall allows light to filter from one room into another. These blocks can be used internally, as shown here, and also in external walls to bring extra natural light into the building.*

windows

Let in the light

Light-giving windows don't deserve to be over-burdened by heavy drapes. Make the most of the light that filters through from the outside with gossamer window treatments.

L ET LIGHT STREAM into your home through windows and glazed doors dressed in sheer fabrics. By keeping window treatments uncomplicated and avoiding heavy drapes, it is not difficult to create a light and airy mood throughout the house. Simple banner curtains and blinds offer little hindrance to daylight, and, depending on the fabric they are made from, they can even be reflective, thus increasing the amount of light inside the house. The first half of this book introduces a range of imaginative window treatments using sheer fabrics that will help to maximize the amount of light coming into your home.

Left (top) *Bright sunshine streams into the room and 'paints' window panes in light onto voile curtains.*

Left (centre) *A tab-headed banner curtain brings privacy to a still-light Shaker-style bathroom.*

Left (bottom) *Light diffusing through a cotton voile curtain has a wonderful, light-giving effect.*

Opposite *This cotton voile offers privacy when the door is open, yet does not obscure too much light.*

Light versus privacy

Few of us are lucky enough to be able to throw open our windows to the world. This is certainly true for bathrooms and bedrooms, and it can apply to living rooms too. The trick is to guard your privacy, while still allowing as much light as possible into the house. It is a delicate balance, but clever use of fabrics can create the desired result.

WHEN THE VIEWS are glorious and your rooms cannot be seen from other buildings, privacy is not your main concern, and you can choose to allow the light in, unfettered even by sheer fabrics hanging at the windows. However, for many city dwellers, the balance between letting in the light and protecting their privacy presents something of a challenge. The traditional solution is to use opaque curtains in conjunction with heavier drapes. However, the modern quest for light, and a reluctance to shroud the windows has led many people to use sheers as their main window dressing.

During the day, while the interior is darker than the exterior, sheer curtains provide as much privacy as traditional opaque curtains. It is later in the evening, when the house is artificially lit, that they may need some help to provide the privacy required. One solution is to fit blinds snug against the window behind the sheers. These can be drawn up and out of sight during the day and then pulled down at night for privacy. Another method is to treat window panes themselves to shield your home from prying eyes. Glass can be stained, sand-blasted, and etched for extra privacy, and these methods can be used with sheer blinds or curtains to create layers of translucency.

There are other light-filtering ways to bring even greater privacy to your home while keeping the window treatments simple. In Georgian times, shutters were cut short to let light in over the top even when they were closed. For a contemporary look, try fitting blinds. These have louvers that can be finely adjusted from fully closed for complete privacy to a horizontal angle that offers a veil of privacy, while allowing

Opposite *Sandblasted glass window panels and a sheer curtain in front of the window allow plenty of light in, yet provide a high degree of privacy.*

plenty of light into the room. Some blinds have finely pierced louvers, which create a pattern of fine pinpricks of light, even when closed. Shutters can be fitted with panels of pierced aluminum or zinc. Pierced aluminum is available in sheet form—large holes let in light while tiny holes offer maximum privacy—so you can select your materials according to your needs.

Louvered wooden shutters provide great flexibility as they can be fitted in sections that can be opened and closed independently and the louvers themselves can also be adjusted. Try them in natural woods or paint them to suit the room. Go as bright as you dare, just think of the glorious painted shutters typical of Caribbean houses. Just make sure that you choose a style that is right for you.

Opposite (top) *A system of three sets of translucent blinds that can be operated independently, teamed with movable solid screens, makes a flexible solution to the need for light and privacy.*

Left (top) *In some cases you may only need to protect your privacy up to eye level. The traditional solution would be to fit a café curtain. This pull-up blind provides a sleek option and still lets direct light through the top of the window.*

Opposite (bottom) *Japanese shoji sliding screens are an effective translucent window treatment that affords plenty of privacy when they are pulled in front of the glass.*

Left (bottom) *Louvered shutters make a smart, timeless treatment that can be adjusted to allow in more or less light.*

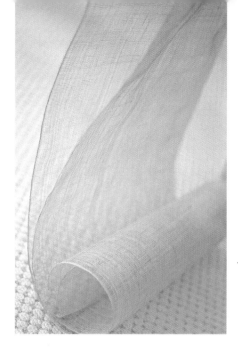

Choosing fabric

There is no need to limit yourself to interior decorator supply stores when looking for sheer fabrics. Try fabric stores, home improvement centers, even secondhand clothiers for delightful materials to dress up your windows.

OST TRANSLUCENT fabrics can be used for sheer window treatments, but the body of the material will make a dramatic difference in the way it hangs, and therefore in the final effect. A fine, soft fabric, like voile, has little body and makes a soft, floaty window treatment, while stiffer organdy will provide a crisper, more tailored look. Check how the fabric handles by gathering the width together in your hand. When you open your hand, the way it springs back will indicate how much body it has. Translucent fabric looks much paler with light flooding through it than it does on the roll, so hold it up to the light before buying. If you are planning to use several different colored materials together in layers, hold them up to the light to see how the shades mix and mingle when daylight is streaming through them.

These are the sheers you're most likely to find:

Butter muslin, or cheesecloth: this inexpensive, loose-weave cotton fabric has coarser threads and less body than other sheers, so coverings look best gathered or pleated.

Madras lace: a soft, pretty cotton lace interwoven with intricate designs. It is often sold in panels.

Organdy: a fine, slightly stiff translucent cotton. It has plenty of body, even after washing.

Organza: this is fine and stiff like organdy, but made from silk. Some are woven with metal; others have designs that incorporate metallic threads. Cheaper, softer organzas are made from polyester, but they do have more body if shot with metal. Always dry clean organza.

Sheer linen: this is fairly expensive but comes in glorious colors and has plenty of body.

Sinamay: a very loose-weave, stiff fabric woven from banana fiber. Good for blinds.

Tulle: this dressmaker's netting makes delightful drapes, but offers minimal privacy.

Voile: this soft, finely-woven fabric can be made of cotton, silk, or polyester. It is best suited for curtains.

Left *When seen on the roll or folded, the colors of sheer fabrics will look much richer than when they are hanging up. These fabrics are (from top) metallic-printed cotton organdy, organza, hand-painted organza, plain white cotton organdy, woven cotton voile, sheer linen, sheer linen with drawn threadwork, natural sinamay with drawn threadwork, dyed sinamay, organza.*

Far left *Sinamay is used to trim hats and its stiffness makes it ideal to use for making blinds.*

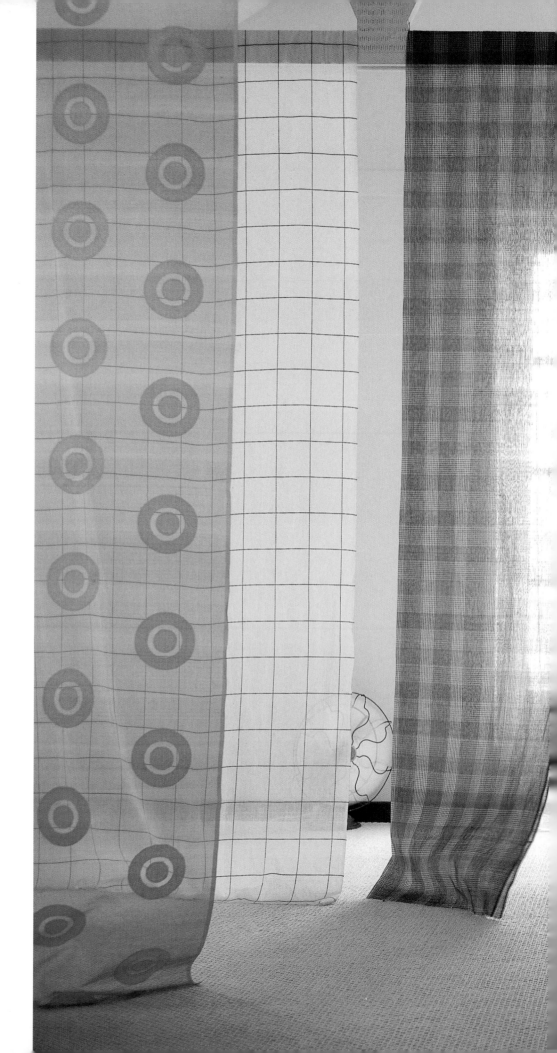

This page *Before buying sheer fabric,*

unroll at least 1¼ yds (1½ m) so

that you can check how it will look

when it's hanging in place. First,

check the color as this will look

considerably different against the

light than it does on the roll. Next,

look at how the fabric drapes. Does it

hang softly, or does it have a stiffness

that will lend extra body to the

finished curtain? If you intend to use

tiebacks with your curtains, or if

you want to drape the fabric in a

particular way, try gathering the fabric

in your hand to re-create the look of

the finished treatment before you buy

to make sure you can achieve the

desired result with your chosen

material. Geometric weaves, such as

these, are a good choice for curtains, as

they have a classic quality that looks

wonderful in both traditional and

more modern homes.

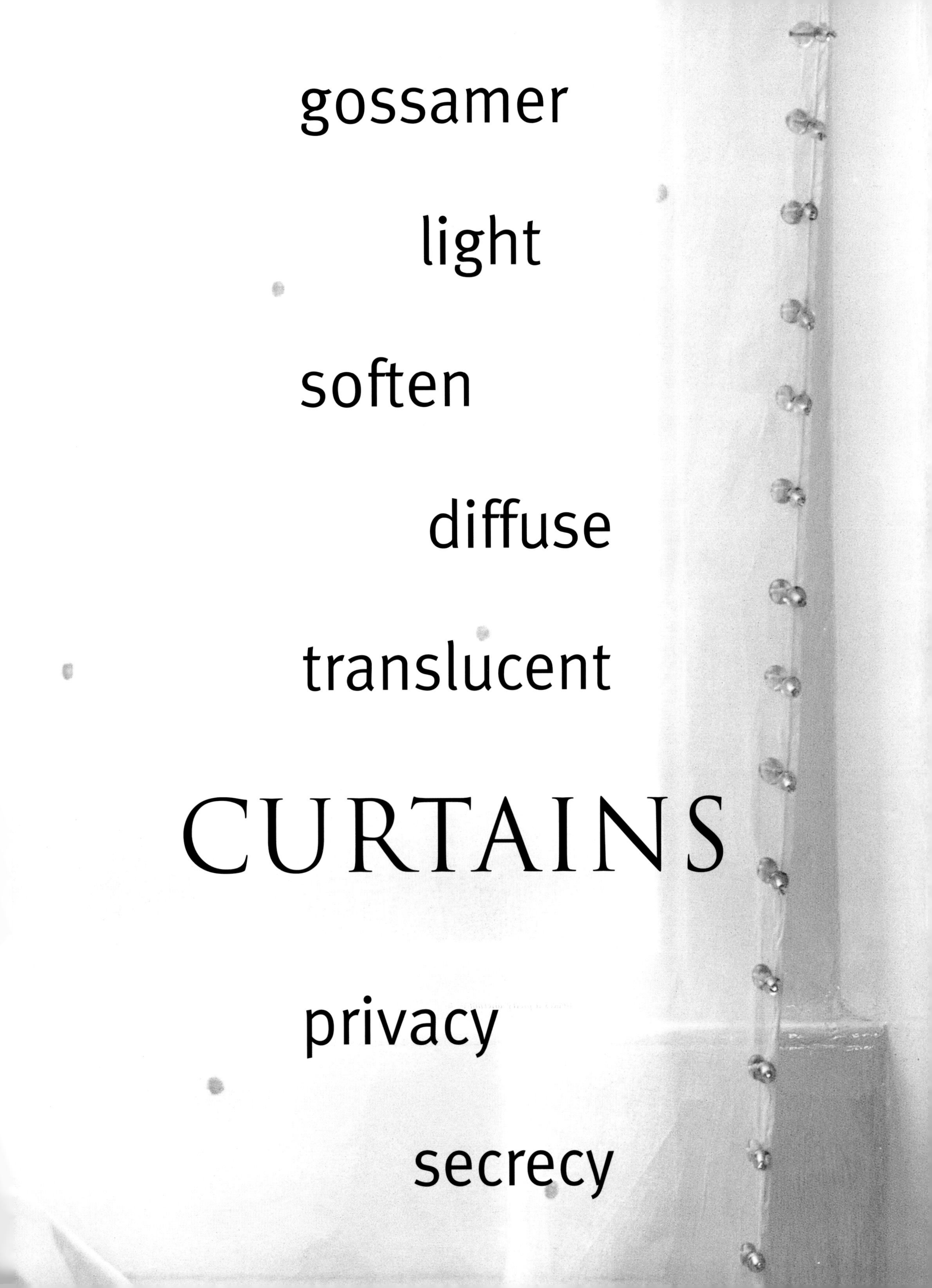

gossamer

light

soften

diffuse

translucent

CURTAINS

privacy

secrecy

Sheer curtains

*Gossamer-light sheers look best hung as
simple banners, free from frills, free from fuss.
Whether you are buying ready-made curtains or
sewing your own, you will find that they will
make a welcome addition to your home.*

WHEN IT COMES to sheers, you need to
forget everything you know about traditional
drapes, whose whole raison d'etre is to lend richness and
warmth to a room. Drapes are traditionally gathered,
pinch- or box-pleated, and, depending on the heading,
they require up to twice the width of the window in
fabric. However, working with sheers is a completely
different matter. Sheers demand much less fuss to show
them off to their best advantage. They look their best
when used as a simple billowing banner. By gathering
the fabrics, you would ruin the look of clean simplicity
that is their very essence. Sheer fabrics simply need to

Left *Soft embroidered cotton voile
makes a pretty alternative to
traditional opaque curtains.*

Right and far right *A soft billowing
panel of Madras lace with an integral
tulip design brings a subtle decorative*

*touch to a sun-drenched window.
This restrained design is unusual
for Madras lace, which can be
quite intricate. The simplicity of
this delicate, textured pattern gives
it a fresh, modern appeal.*

be cut a little wider than the window to allow for some movement, so that the finished window treatment looks simple without being too stingy.

There is no need to line sheers since lining only cuts out the light, diminishing their diaphanous quality. At all costs, avoid the temptation of lining them with a cheap voile or cheesecloth. These have little body and simply add weight to the curtain, resulting in a window treat–ment that lacks the necessary luxurious feel. If you do choose one of the softer sheers (such as a fine voile) for your curtains, you can add extra body by hanging it in layers or using box pleats.

The emerging popularity of sheers means that in addition to a wider choice of interesting fabrics to buy on the roll, more and more home furnishing stores are offer-ing inexpensive ready-made sheers. Many are available with tabs ready to hang on a curtain rod, others are sold simply as panels. To hang these, you need curtain clips which come fixed to a ring or hooks that slips onto a rod or wire. You then attach them to the top of the curtain. Ready-made sheers are a real gift for people who do not have the time or inclination to make their own curtains. However, you can still individualize a ready-made curtain using a variety of trimmings, such as ribbon, braid, or beads. Even more ordinary household materials, such as string, buttons, and curtain weights, can be striking.

Sheer curtains can be made using patterned fabrics or plains, and in a variety of colors, using whatever additions or trimmings you like. Try to choose trimmings that are in keeping with the room's decorative style.

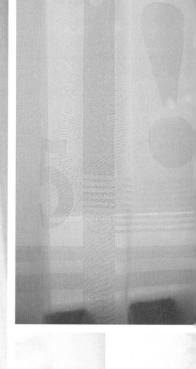

This image *The tulip motifs have been woven onto a basic cotton weave, which is typical of Madras lace. Other designs are more intricate, often consisting of an overall design that also has sections of drawn threadwork. Traditionally made as window panels, Madras lace was never designed to be gathered. With the current fashion for sheers, these panels have a new-found popularity.*

Right *These three variations of cotton voile have subtle, woven-in self designs that show the variety of patterns that are available.*

(top) *Feminine florals are always popular for soft furnishings.*

(middle) *Sleek, contemporary designs give a wonderful modern look to the room and make a bold statement.*

(bottom) *Subtle, stylish patterns will always have a place in interior design.*

Right *India is one of the traditional suppliers of textiles to the world. The country is now manufacturing some exquisite ready-made curtain panels to Western specifications. This elegant curtain is made up of three sections (taupe/cream/taupe) that have been joined together with smart, double top-stitched seams. This geometric pattern has a classic look that is versatile enough to look at home anywhere, from a traditional country-style setting to the sleekest city apartment. The subtle pattern adds extra visual interest at a large window, without overwhelming the architecture. Wider than the window, the taupe sections have been folded toward the middle white section to make a smart treatment that has plenty of body.*

Little additions

You don't have to be a confident seamstress to create beautiful, unique curtains for your home. It couldn't be easier to adapt a ready-made curtain and make it into something really special.

IT REALLY ISN'T difficult to sew inexpensive trimmings onto tab-headed, ready-made curtains, yet the finished effect is both elegant and delightful.

To over-embellish a simple window panel would destroy its intrinsic beauty. Instead, try to think of ways to add interest that complement, rather than overwhelm, the original curtain. It is a good idea to use trimmings that are similar in tone to the original fabric. Sheer fabrics are translucent, so they will always appear lighter once they are in place at the window, and a trimming that is much darker than the main fabric will look too heavy. Translucent or fine trimmings look lovely because the light can pass through them in the same way as through the body of the panel, so glass beads make ideal trimmings. Feathers look equally effective for the same reason. Alternatively you can choose a light-reflective detail, such as pearl or shell buttons, which will catch the light when the curtain is hung in place. Let your imagination run wild to create a look that is just right for you and your home.

This page and opposite

Glass beads catch the

light bringing sparkle to

the edges of a crisp,

white, cotton organdy

panel. The appeal lies in

the play of light on the

organdy and the glass,

both of which reflect

brightness into the room.

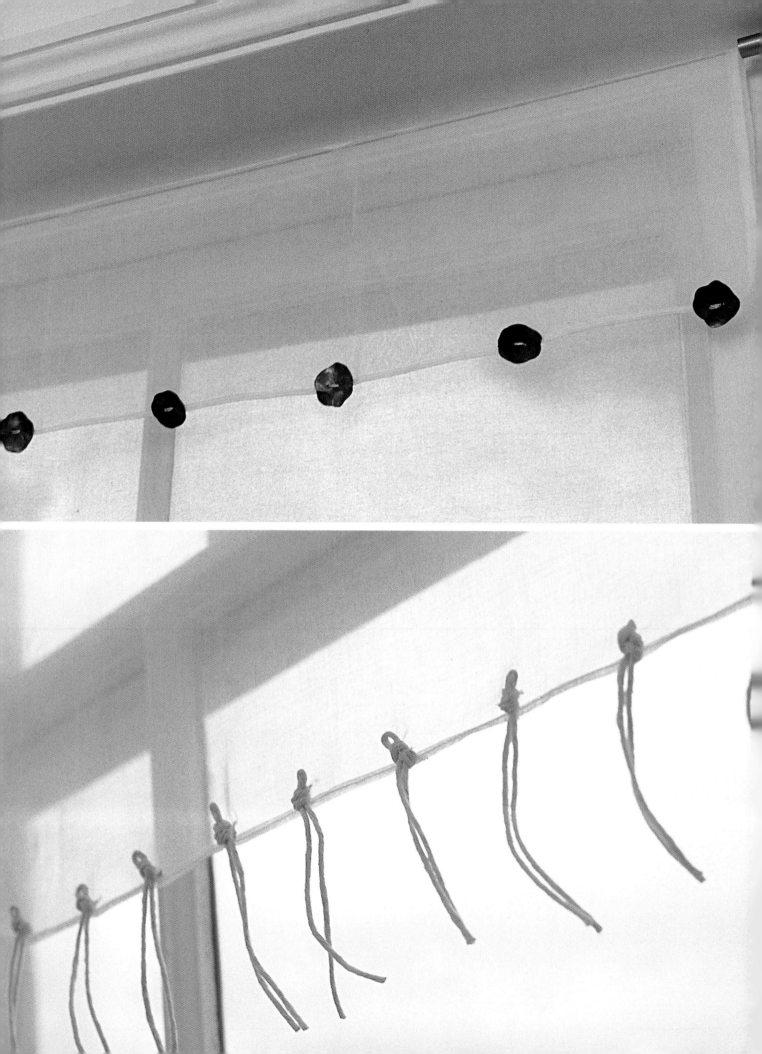

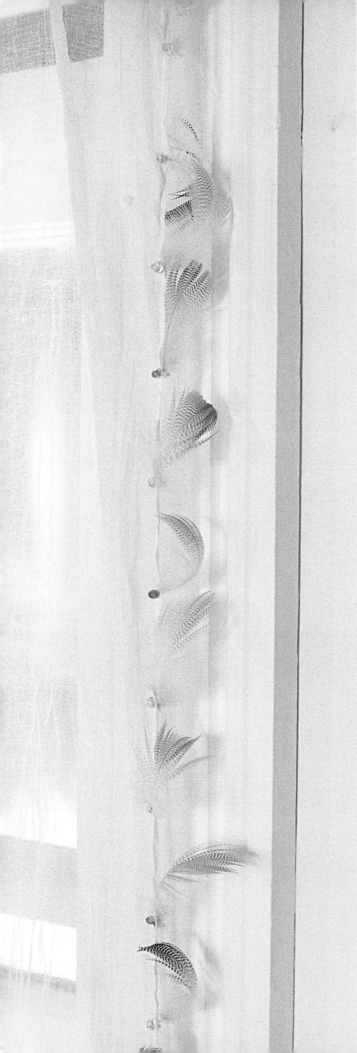

Alternative edgings

Opposite (top) *Simple, restrained decorations make humble components look elegant. Here, the button-like edgings are actually basic curtain weights that have been hammered for a soft, textured effect. Widely spaced, and stitched to the narrow hems of a simple, pure-white organdy panel, these edgings look deceptively expensive.*

Opposite (bottom) *Household string makes a surprisingly smart fringing that is perfect for sheers when each piece is set well apart from its neighbor. Always use pure cotton string as that will hang obediently without taking on awkward kinks or unraveling too readily. Cut it into lengths. Fold one in half, then tie a simple knot, leaving a loop at the top to let through the light and give an overall feeling of lightness. When all the strings are knotted, stitch them into position, using an easy measure, such as the three fingers of your left hand, to space them. As a finishing touch, trim the tassels to even lengths.*

Left *Light and floaty, yet surprisingly robust, feathers make a delightful trimming for sheer curtains or blinds. Their see-through quality enhances the translucence of the fabric, and provides an unusual visual focus for the window treatment. Simply sew the feathers on by spearing the quill with the needle, then add a tiny glass bead to each feather for extra shine and to help keep the feather in place. Stitch them firmly into position. When laundering sheers with washable trimmings, put the curtain in a pillowcase before washing or dry cleaning to avoid damaging either your washing machine or the curtain.*

Edging with color

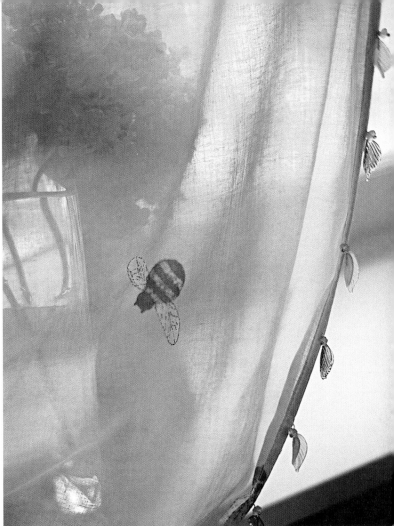

Opposite *Pretty printed voile sheers look charming when partnered with glass bead trimmings. Here, alternating clear and frosted glass leaf beads add sparkle, yet complement the color of the curtain. When choosing trimmings for sheer curtains, remember that the color of the fabric will look very different when it is hanging at the window than it appears on the roll. For this reason it is important that you take some of the fabric with you when you are choosing the trimmings. Hold the fabric and the trimming up to the light to get a better idea of what the finished effect will be.*

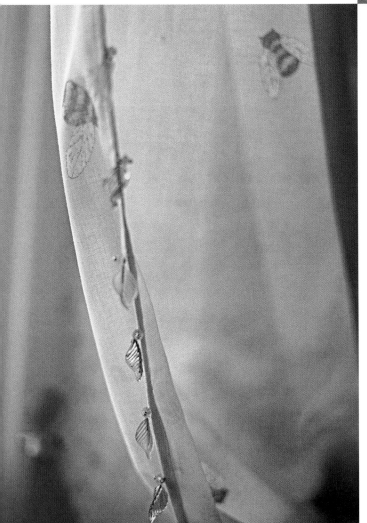

Above *When the curtains are tucked into tiebacks, the leaves take on a different quality and appear to float down like autumn leaves. The alternating frosted and clear leaves add tonal variation, mimicking the real thing.*

Left *Delicate trimmings such as glass beads look best when sewn to curtains with the smallest, neatest possible hems. Fortunately, with fine cotton voile, this is not difficult to do. The easiest method is to press in a tiny single turning, then press this over before attempting to machine stitch the fabric. The leaf beads incorporate a little metal loop for sewing on. Attach this to the fabric, then add a tiny frosted blue flower and seed bead, both to add charm and to keep the leaf firmly in place on the curtain. These tiny, delicate trimmings look delightful when the sunlight shines through the window and onto the curtain.*

Clever paneling

Translucent paneled curtains create an ethereal look, but because all the workings are on show, seams must be neat. This is not difficult and the seams can become a decorative feature.

S HEER, FLOATY ORGANZAS look wonderful seamed together using a robust jeans seaming. This makes a neat fray-free finish that can be turned into a feature, as here, with gold top-stitching. Once you've mastered the technique, you will be able to use even the narrowest of fabrics and seam them together to create your own designs. Use vertical seams, as here, for an elegant look that can improve the proportion of your windows; try horizontal seams; or even organza patchwork for a more lively, fun effect. Dress fabric departments are ideal hunting grounds for glorious metal-shot organzas, which can be made up into diaphanous curtains, or look in Indian markets for exotic gold-embroidered sari fabrics.

Left *Organza, hand painted with filigree-fine florals, makes pretty sheers. Plain panels are seamed on either side for an uncluttered look.*

Far left (top) *Vertical panels make elegant curtains, elongating the proportions of the windows.*

Far left (bottom) *The curtain is clipped to a tension wire with simple metal clips (curtain clips with the rings removed) for an easy, unobtrusive heading.*

Alternative seaming to try **Above (left)** *Turn seams on translucent fabrics into a feature. Here, the widths have been joined using tiny French seams,*

then pintucks have been put in between the seams. **Above (center)** *Here, French seams have been turned into a diamond pattern by running parallel lines of stitching across the*

French seams, which have been turned inward for one line, outward for the next, and so on. **Above (right)** *Loose-weave fabrics, such as sheer linen, look wonderful when the edges*

are frayed. So make a feature of it by stitching one panel on top of the other, about 4 in. (10 cm) from the raw edge, then fray that edge for a soft, feathery look.

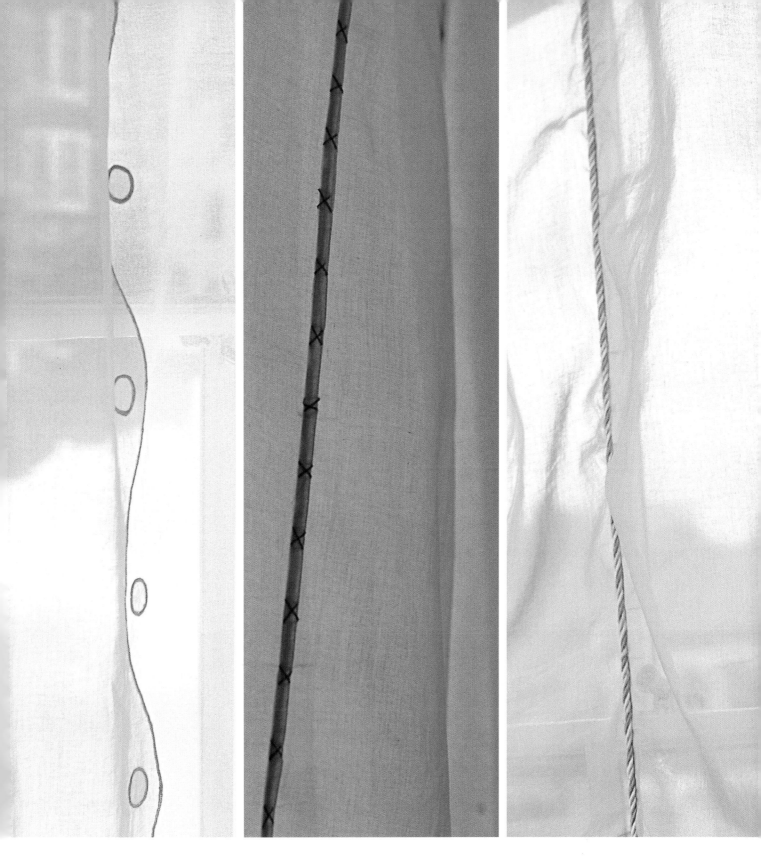

Alternative seaming to buy

Above (left) *Don't worry if your sewing skills are limited. Designers are waking up to the increasing interest in combining sheer fabrics. Many eye-catching designs of ready-seamed contrasting fabrics are now available to buy on the roll. Cream and lime, joined by wavy lines will give any room a fresh, youthful feel.* **Above (center)** *Delightful peachy combinations with hand-embroidered crosses down the seams provide extra visual interest.* **Above (right)** *Citrus shades seamed together, then trimmed with two-tone cord will bring a splash of summer to any climate.*

Hanging sheers

Featherlight sheers make little demand on the headings or hardware needed to hang them, so don't worry about weight-bearing capabilities. You are free to make your choice entirely on looks!

COMPLEMENT YOUR TRANSLUCENT sheers with supports that reflect the light, such as rods in polished steel or nickel, or choose a smart minimal solution such as a tension wire. These supports are now available in kit form from interior shops, and are inexpensive and easy to put up. Another solution is a line of hooks fixed into the door or window molding—so the curtains can simply be hooked into position. Headings, too, can be lightweight. Tabs, ties, eyelets, and hooks usually look best on sheers, and some deceptively simple solutions, such as string or bulldog clips, can look striking. As always, think about the whole look that you want to create in the room, and choose hardware that enhances, rather than competes with, sheer fabric.

Top *Organza looks exquisite threaded onto a stainless steel pole. Make a deep double or triple hem before adding the eyelets to prevent the fabric from pulling away from the metal.*

Bottom *Slim ties, added to complement the check in the fabric, make a pretty heading that lends a feeling of lightness at the top of the curtain.*

Top *Tension wires are neat and unobtrusive and can easily support the weight of the curtain. Fix the end part of the brackets first, and screw the wires into position with the front part of the bracket until they are taut. This system originates from yachting wires, but now many interior stores have come up with their own version. Here, simple curtain clips are used to hang the fabric on the wire.*
Center *These shells add a glorious natural feel to any drape. They come on special hooks that have a double bend in the wire—one for the shell and one for the curtain. Punch holes in the top of the curtain and hook it in place.* **Bottom** *Curtain rings, hooks and clips are linked together to create a fancy metal heading that adds a delicate lightness to these printed voile curtains.*

Top *Shoestring ties in palest pink cotton organdy are fixed to wrought-iron hooks to create a feminine effect. This elegant curtain heading clearly demomstrates that you do not always need fancy, expensive trimmings and hardware to achieve a beautiful look. This simple treatment is just right for this delicate, sheer fabric.*

Right *White glass droplets add a charming decorative touch to the curtains. Here, they are shown to their best advantange hanging in front of simple, specially designed curtain hooks. Once you begin to experiment with different headings and hardware, you will probably find yourself looking at everyday objects as potential trimmings or hangings for a window treatment. Ready-made hardware cannot compete with your own imagination.*

Top *Even the most prosaic items can look smart if they are chosen with care. This heading is made up of ordinary bulldog clips. Fix them over the tension wire and clip onto a ready-made panel. This quick and easy solution is, nevertheless, extremely smart.*

Center *Headings need not be elaborate or expensive. Here, pure cotton organdy paneled curtains have been headed with simple household cotton string to great effect.*

Bottom *Here, basic curtains have been hemmed, given a heading of tiny eyelets and hung on tension wire. Nothing could be simpler, or more exquisite. These clean, simple lines are ideal for a room with a sleek modern decorating scheme, where more complicated treatments would look out of place.*

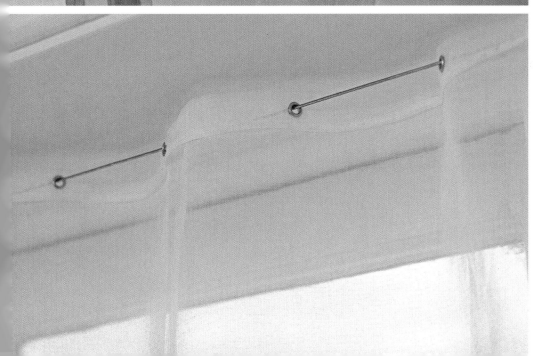

Draping sheers

The translucency of sheers affects their overall look when they are draped because all the folds, layer upon layer, are in full view, making a delightful play on light and shadow.

DIAPHANOUS FABRICS LOOK best when draped with simplicity. Too much gathering or elaborate ruching can become over-fussy because every tiny tuck is in full view through the translucency of the folds. Simple banners look exquisite. They are at their best when they are just a little wider than the window, as that gives them some movement and depth. The lightweight quality of sheer fabric offers all sorts of ways to drape that would be impossible with any other fabric. Curtains can be given one huge knot in the middle, or two can be knotted together, creating natural, unfussy gathers that cast glorious patterns of light and shadow.

For a more traditional style, you can simply drape sheers over a pole, and being so lightweight, they can be relied upon to stay in place without fastening. Alternatively, two differently colored fabrics can be hung from one pole and allowed to overlap in places. The transparency of the fabric means that where the colors overlap, they appear to mix to create a glorious medley of shades. Spend some time experimenting with your chosen fabrics until you achieve the desired effect.

Above *A pair of cotton organdy curtains are knotted in the middle to create a delightful pattern of light and shade. The natural stiffness of organdy lends body to the folds. A finer voile would not work as well.*

Above *Clever draping onto a simple curtain wire*

transforms a long thin embroidered Indian head-

shawl into a delightful sheer window treatment.

Above *A slim cord knotted around the fine,*

embroidered fabric creates gentle folds for added

interest and depth.

Above *A translucent jacket hung on a simple wire coat hanger forms a*

glorious, sculptural window treatment. It works because it acts as a veil

at the window, rather than as a mask.

Above *Inspired by box pleats on a skirt, the colored panels on this*

certain have been pulled over the central white panel to create an

extremely simple, yet smart, tailored look.

Above *Traditional draping looks extremely elegant when carried out with restraint. Here, a length of fabric has been brought up and over an antique*

pole, across the front and down over the pole again. The key to the success of this treatment is that the hanging width of fabric is not much wider than

the window, and so the fabric does not fall into too many gathers and spoil the simple look.

Appliqué

Simple shapes are the hallmarks of modern appliqué. Apply them to basic sheer curtain panels to make delightful, yet practical, works of art that are tailor-made for your windows.

T RADITIONALLY, APPLIQUÉ IS used to add intricate pattern to a main fabric, but it can be much simpler than that. Even geometric shapes as basic as squares and rectangles are perfectly respectable as appliqué motifs. If they are cut to elegant proportions and carefully positioned on a sheer panel, they can create a smart, modern look. The key to working with appliqué in this way is to think of the whole panel as a blank canvas to decorate, and then to cut and arrange the pieces to provide a pleasing overall balance. Before you begin, first draw up a plan to scale, cutting out the appliqué pieces in paper so that you can play about with their sizes and positions before cutting.

Sheer fabrics provide an added dimension to appliqué by the very nature of their translucency. Extra layers, even of the same fabric, can produce a shimmery quality where the weaves interact. Add new colors, one on top of the other; being transparent, they combine to make a wealth of new colors and tones. Try different fabrics to see what effects you can achieve.

Right *This exquisite curtain panel has a French feel. Here, simple, square*

pockets have been applied to the curtain and skeletonized leaves tucked in.

Previous page and above *Slim ties in a soft feminine pink, fixed in bows onto wrought-iron hooks, make a pretty heading that does not overwhelm the simple curtain. The method of hanging that you choose is just as important as your choice of fabric. All too often a lovely window treatment is spoiled by the wrong hooks or rod. As the curtain above shows, curtain hardware need not be expensive. Here, the simplest and probably least expensive option is undoubtedly the best choice for the situation. The plain hooks offer a timeless simplicity that gives the panel a light, airy feel. A more structured or ornate rod could have been too dominant.*

Above *Appliqué can be more than just geometric pieces of fabric sewn onto a background. Here, magnolia leaves provide an attractive alternative. First the leaves were arranged on the panel to form a pleasing design, then the pockets were cut to fit the leaves. Anything could be put into the pockets, but translucent items look best with sheer materials as they let the light stream through. Solid items would appear as a black shape on sunny days. Think about how you could personalize the curtains. Try feathers or shapes cut from contrasting sheers or pieces of lace as alternatives to the skeletonized leaves.*

Alternative appliqué

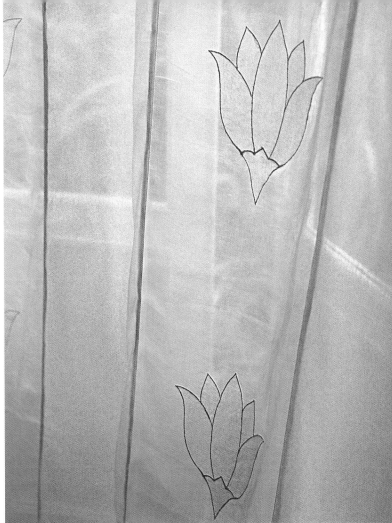

Opposite *Here, a pair of curtains and top panel combine to form an overall "canvas" at the window with rectangles and strips of toning and contrasting colors running across the boundaries. Hung at doors which overlook the ocean, the main fabric is a sheer linen, a translucent fabric that has plenty of body, yet offers more weight than many other sheer fabrics. Appliquéd rectangles of fine metal-shot organzas in green and pink meet and cross each other across the whole window, bringing a little sparkle and subtle color changes where they mingle to complement the sea view beyond.*

Above *Glorious appliquéd curtains can be very simple to make, even if your sewing skills are limited. Some breathtaking ready-appliquéd fabrics are available on the roll. This one consists of panels of taupe and cream fabric seamed together with elegant lotus flowers ready-appliquéd to the cream fabric. All you need to do is simply to cut the various fabrics to length, hem all the sides, then hang the curtain on a rod or wire using curtain clips.*

Left *The way in which light plays upon nature's forms, adapting and changing the colors, can provide inspiration for color combinations in appliqué in the same way as it does for an artist. Just think of the number of shades of green you can see on one, solitary tree. Here, the greens and yellows of the pears provide subtle color combinations that complement the blue curtain.*

Sheer ribbon curtains

Delicate organdy ribbons, simply tied to a curtain rail, make a delightful no-sew curtain. Use two or three colors to create a delicate striped effect.

This page *Floating gently in the breeze, these knotted fabrics soften the hard, square edges of a plain, white window frame.*

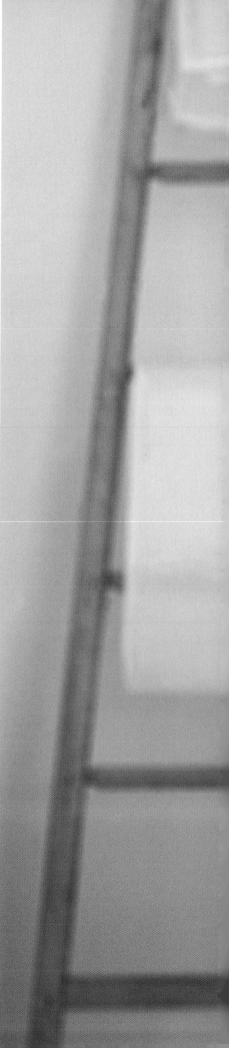

Don't stop at the fabrics when you are looking for curtain materials. You can use anything that dresses the window, softens less-than-beautiful views and creates a feature in the room. Seek out ribbons, tapes, and cords then slip on a few beads or coins with holes in the center collected from holidays abroad. Try strings of beads or a length of mesh, such as sina-may, with sections trimmed with beads or feathers. The idea is to protect your privacy, yet let as much light into the room as you can. This minimal treatment will also complement the innate beauty of the architecture while softening any stark lines within the room.

This page *Less is more when decorating an attractive molding. Try to accentuate, rather than overwhelm, the shape and form of the window by using sheer organdy ribbon for a pretty, yet unobtrusive dressing.*

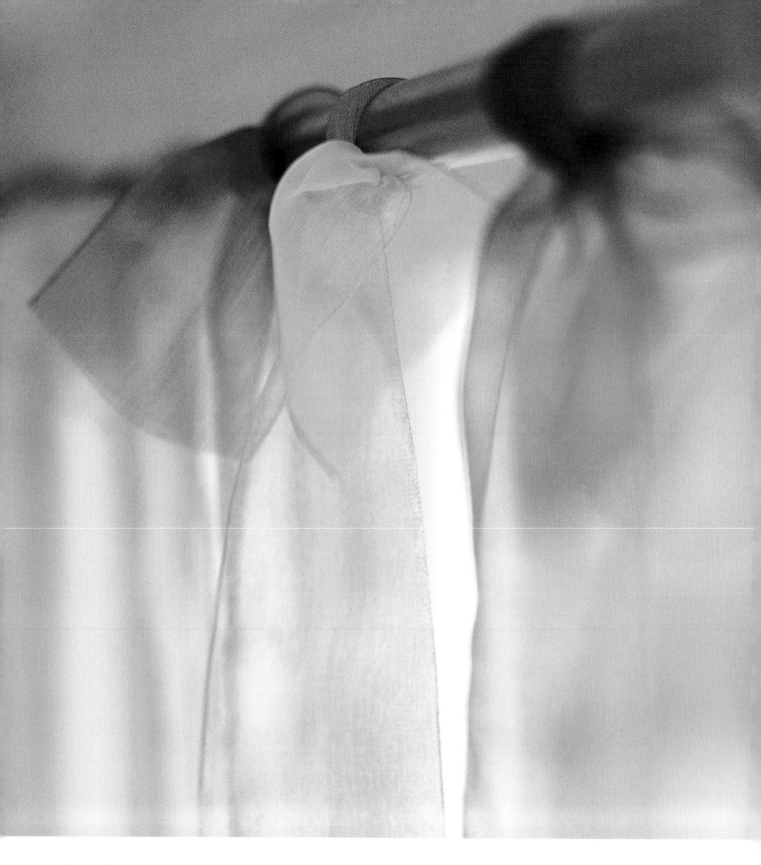

Above *Headings need not be complicated or expensive to be effective. Here, the ribbons are simply tied onto a metal pole. Tie the ribbons on, leaving about 6 in. (15 cm) free,*

to make a soft and pretty feature at the top of the curtain. The extra ribbon gives the curtain a fuller, more billowing look, yet it does not spoil the overall simple, flowing effect.

Note the way that the fresh, watery colors of the layers interact to create an exquisite effect that positively invites sunlight into the room. This simple, but rather glamorous,

curtain would look quite at home in any room in the house.

Above *The combination of alternating aqua and green sheer ribbon flooded with light gives a wonderful watery feel. Experiment with the relationship between colors by holding your fabrics up to the light, and moving them around until you achieve the look you want.*

Above *Tie a knot at the end of each ribbon to give it a little weight, intensify the colors and to lend interest to the overall window treatment. Anything that creates layers in the fabric will have an interesting visual effect, and changing the weight of the curtain will affect the way it moves.*

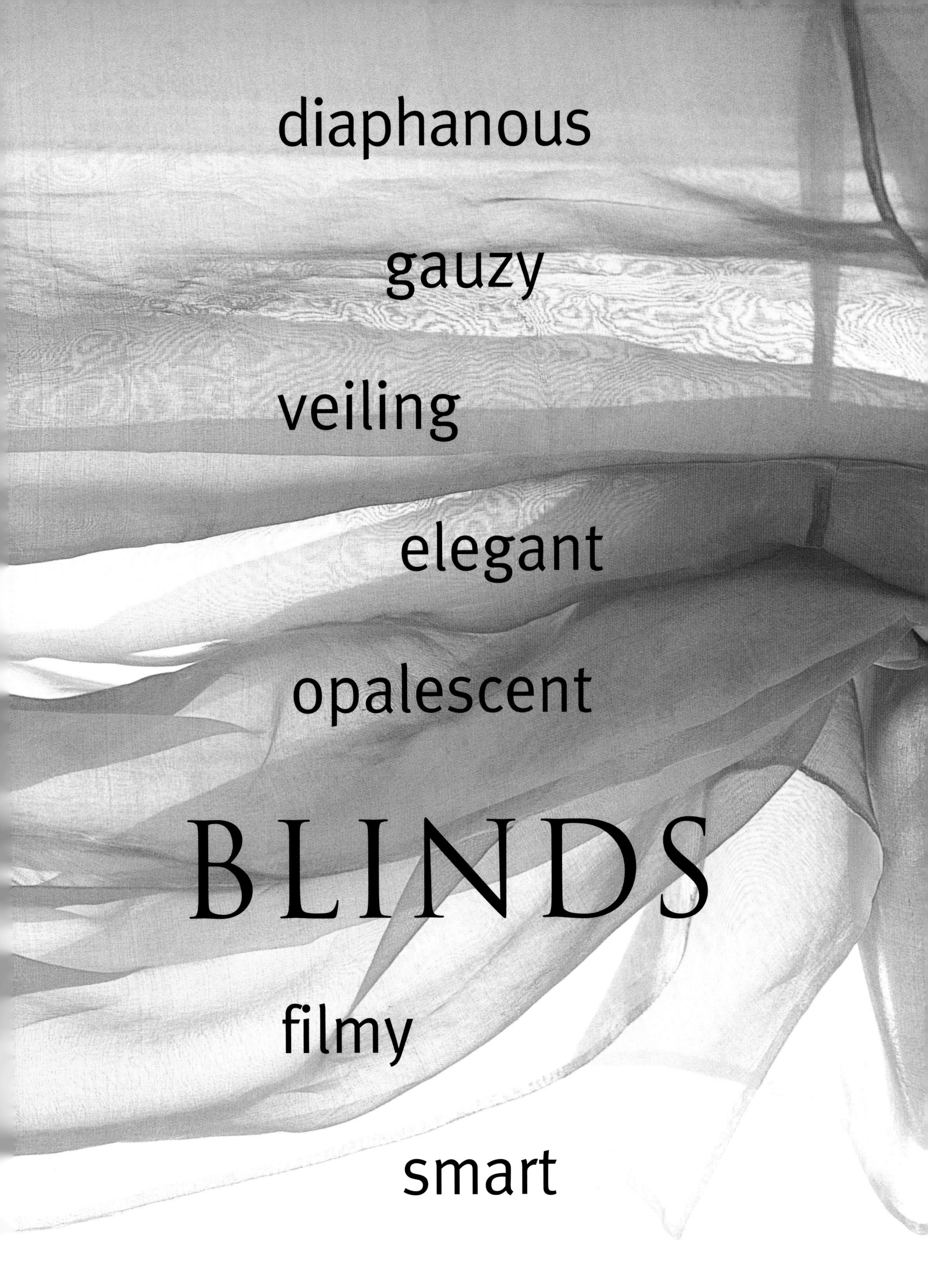

diaphanous

gauzy

veiling

elegant

opalescent

BLINDS

filmy

smart

Choosing blinds

Blinds make a wonderful partner for elegant architecture. Light-diffusing

or light-filtering, they are easily adjusted to let plenty of light into the room

when required, or to create a degree of much-needed privacy. Use them

throughout your home for a smart, tailored look.

SHEER BLINDS DIFFUSE the light and look elegant, but, like all blinds, they do require some sewing skills. You need to approach making them in a slightly different way to making blinds from regular furnishing fabric (this is dealt with in detail on pages 66-77).

There is also a wide choice available to buy. Roller shades pull down, then roll back up when you release the rewind mechanism; woven wood or matchstick blinds are pulled up and released on a pulley system; Roman blinds fold up neatly; and London blinds loosely concertina for a softer look. Floor-mounted blinds can be pulled up to cover the window. These are ideal for ground floors as they can be pulled up to just above eye-level for privacy, but allow light to come in over the top. If they are made of sheer fabrics, blinds are light diffusing, letting light into the room while protecting your privacy. Venetian and louvered blinds are made of solid materials such as wood or aluminum, but have louvers that can be opened to let light in. Some have finely pierced louvers which allow light through even when closed.

This page and top left *Although it is basically opaque, the fabric of this blind is actually a form of cutwork, which lets undiffused light into the room. The effect is very chic.*

Top right *Wooden slatted Venetian blinds can be adjusted to regulate the light coming into the room.*

Bottom left *A neat Roman blind gives a sophisticated look. Here,*

the simple lines of the blind are ideal for this tiny bedroom.

Bottom right *Simple canvas reefed blinds make a smart, uncluttered statement in a simple room.*

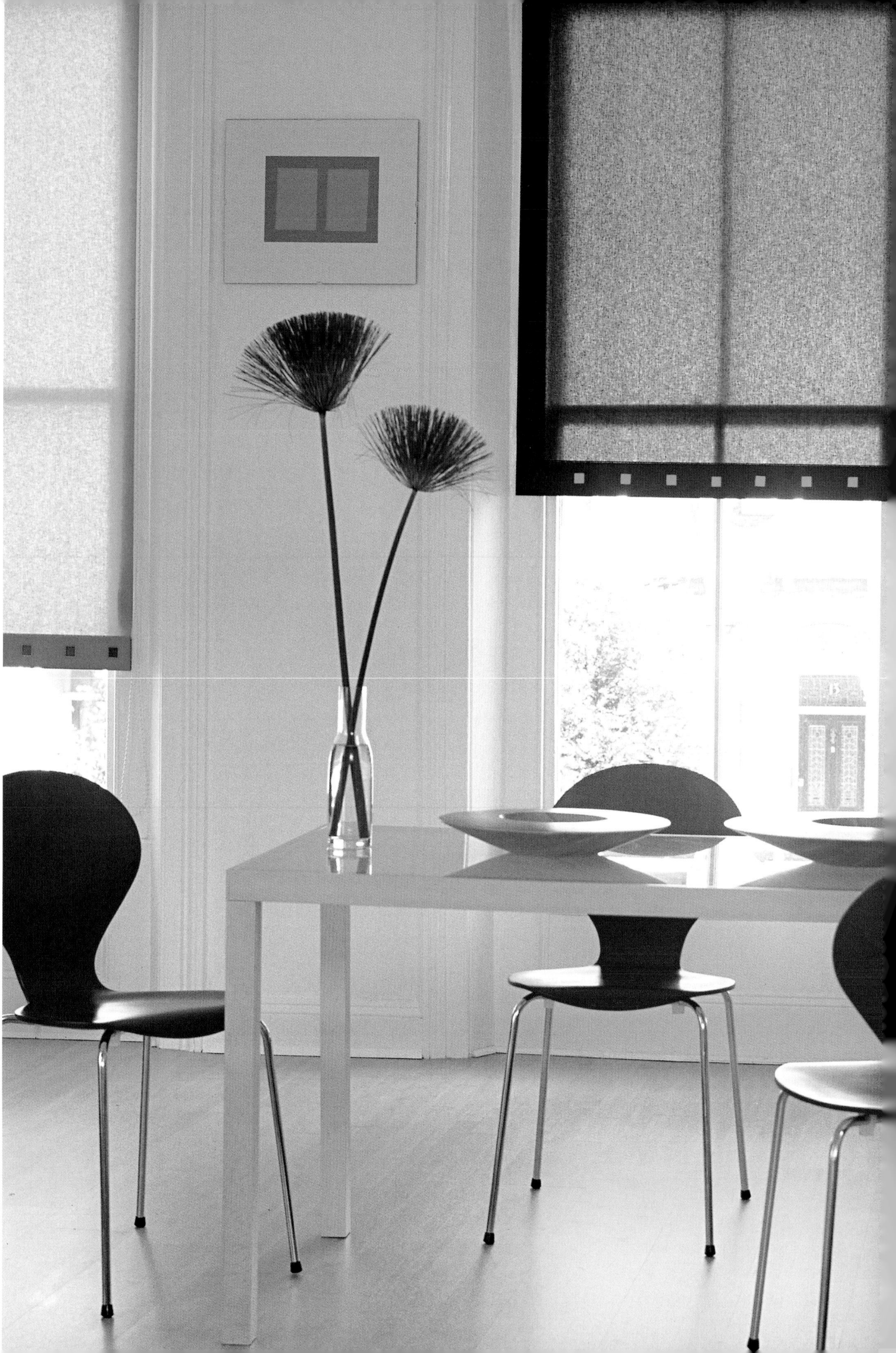

Left *Sheer fabrics do not have to be limited to pale, delicate colors. Stronger shades can be used to create a clean, quite contemporary effect. Here, a trio of deep-toned cotton roller shades bring color to an elegant, pure-white room. The loose weave of these blinds ensures that the light is still diffused, softening the tones as it does. The choice of the hardware for the blind has an important role to play in creating the look as well. The bottom bars are made of Plexiglas, which lets in windows of light through the squares cut in the fabric to make a smart edging. There is a wide choice of ready-made and made-to-measure roller shades on the market. Since the fabric for these requires considerable stiffening, the very finest sheer fabrics are not really suitable for these kinds of blinds. Choose fabrics that have plenty of body for the best effect.*

Details that count

When blinds are sheer their workings are on show, and solid materials look black against the light. Seek out beautiful alternatives and make sure that your seams are always neat.

T RANSPARENCY IS DEMANDING because you cannot hide the "wrong side." The back needs to be as beautiful as the front, so pay as much attention to the choice of materials for the "workings" of the blind as you do to the main fabrics. As well as beautiful linings, you need to think about cords, rings, and (for Roman blinds) supports. Traditional heavy battens, utility cords and rings could spoil the delicate look that you are trying to achieve. You do not have to venture far to find the right materials—your local fabric store should suffice.

Left (top) *Make the smallest French seams possible for a neat, fray-free appearance that becomes part of the design.* **Left (bottom)** *A pure white cotton organdy was used to line this organza blind. Blue organdy ribbons show through to the front and make attractive substitute cords.*

Center (top) *Metallic dress stays make an attractive alternative to wooden battens.* **Center (bottom)** *Metallic ribbon coordinates with the stays.* **Right (top)** *Even at the back, the blind looks beautiful.*

Right (bottom) *White swans' quills make elegant "battens."*

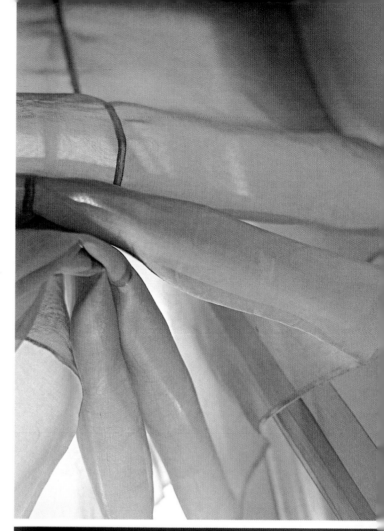

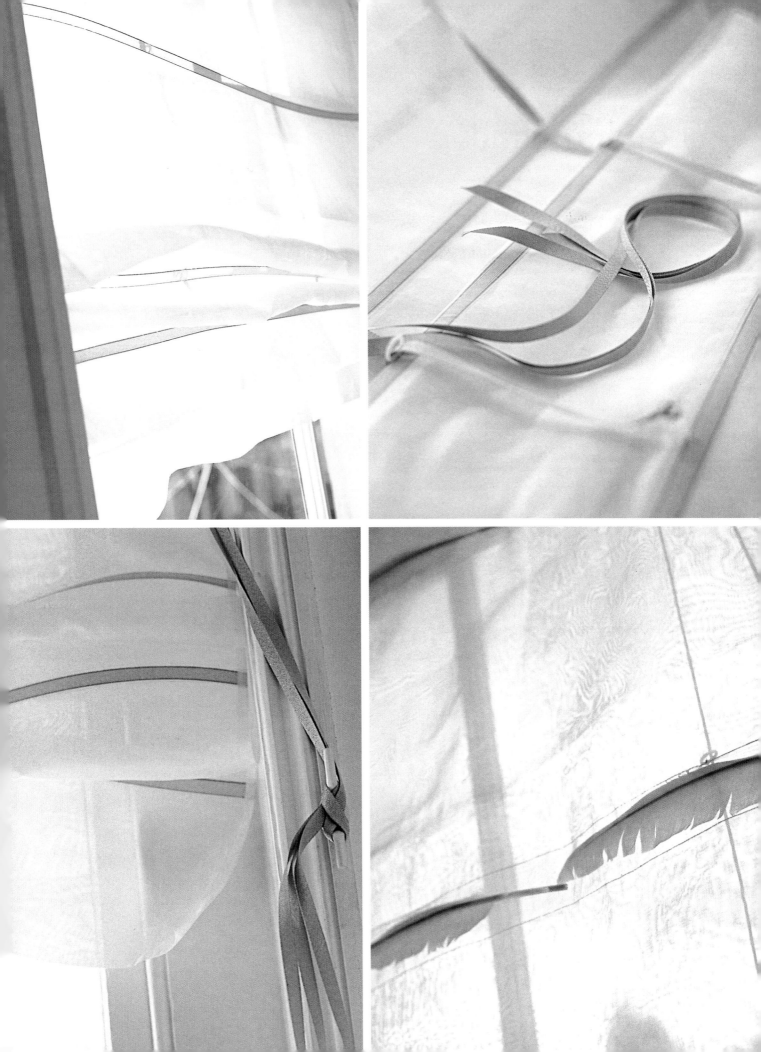

London blinds

The translucent quality of a sheer London blind means that seaming, linings, and pull-up cords are there for all to see, even from the front, so choose the material with care.

THIS SHEER VERSION of a classic blind draws up into soft folds. Sheer blinds must be lined in order to support their working mechanisms. However, the lining fabric must have at least as much translucency and reflectiveness as the front fabric in order to retain its diaphanous quality. The safest solution is to self-line the blind, although you can mix fabrics if you're careful. Lining a green metal-shot organza fabric with a white cotton organdy creates a fabulous double shadow effect in the folds. It works because both fabrics are highly translucent and light reflective. When buying, hold both fabrics up to natural daylight to check the effect.

Left (top) *Blue organza ribbon complements the shot metallic blind.*

Left (bottom) *Light-reflective white cotton organdy used as the lining gives the blind body without obliterating any of its translucency.*

Center *Fine French seams joining the fabric widths, seen through the blind, become part of the design.*

Far right *The use of exquisite materials makes the reverse side as beautiful as the front.*

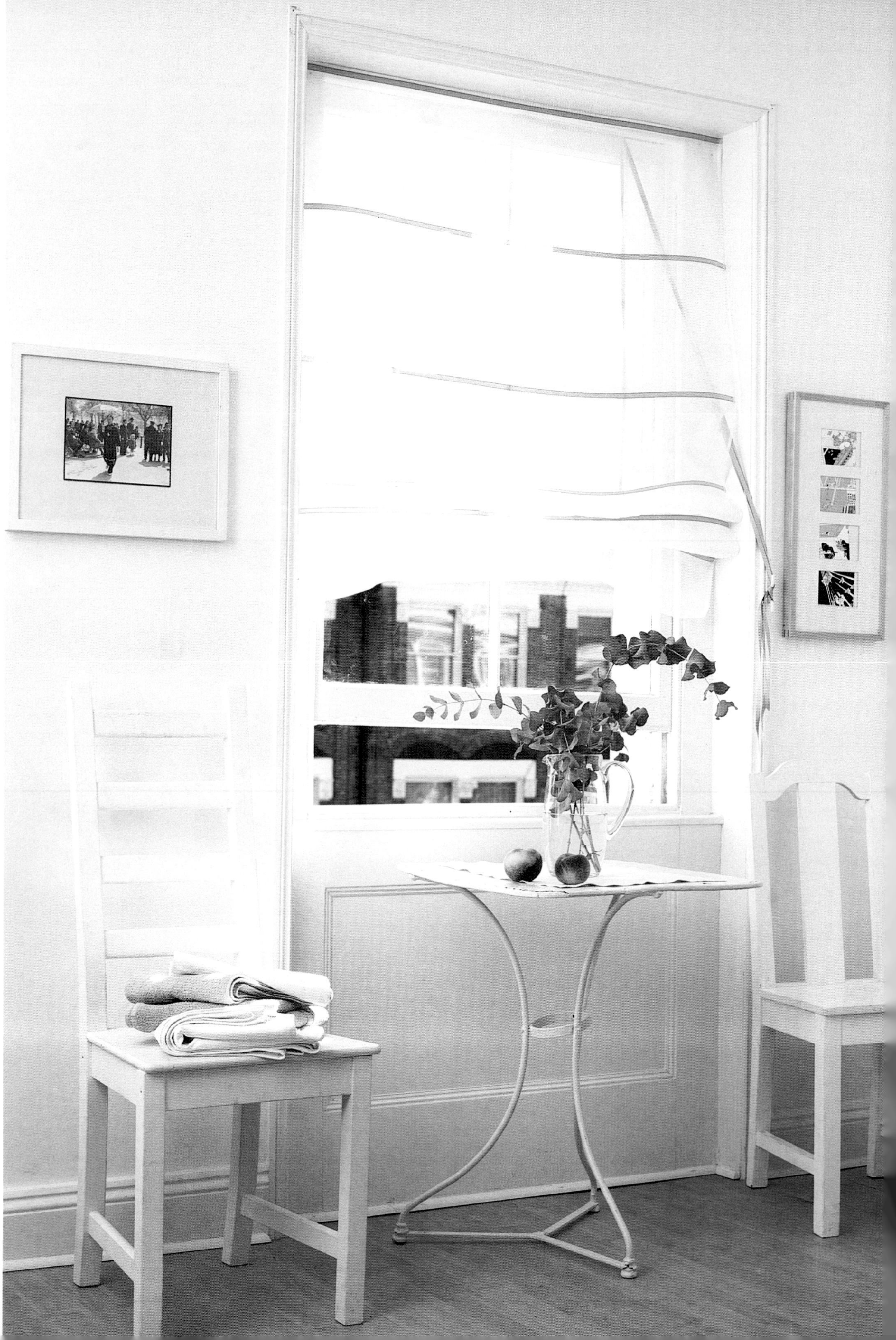

Supports with style

Since the battens on sheer Roman blinds are visible, the best solution is to make them into an attractive feature. Even the underpinnings of these translucent blinds need to be beautiful.

S HEER ROMAN BLINDS require a little lateral thinking because delicate, transparent fabrics provide no cover for ugly supporting battens. The trick is to think of the hardware as another decorative feature of the blind. The beautiful metallic strip used here is actually lingerie "boning." This is usually made in white plastic and sold by the length, but, you can also buy this delightful, light-reflective silvery version that has been intended for designers and makers of translucent garments. The overall effect of the metallic supports, creating smart stripes through the simple, white organdy, was so stunning that the supports were used as an intrinsic part of the final design. Set at ever increasing distances apart, they add dynamism to the finished look of this simple, smart blind.

Left *Highly reflective pure white cotton organdy is shown to its best advantage by silvery supporting battens and ribbon pulls. These workings complement, rather than overwhelm, this delicate blind.*

Right (top) *Even the sheerest organdy effectively softens a dominant cityscape.*

Right (bottom) *When the blind is fully let down, the metallic stays create an attractive, striped look.*

Feather supports

Naturally elegant pure-white swans' quills have been used in rows of three to form the support system for this Roman blind. They become an integral part of the overall design. The translucency of feathers makes them ideal companions for delicate, sheer fabrics.

EXQUISITE SUPPORTS FOR sheer Roman blinds can be found in all kinds of unlikely places. A single swan's quill found by the local pond was the inspiration for this blind. It seemed ideal: lightweight yet strong, light filtering and white, which would complement perfectly the white organdy. If finding enough suitable white quills proves impractical, look up suppliers of feathers to the fashion industry.

Sheer Roman blinds differ from their opaque counterparts in more ways than just their translucency and need for beautiful supports. Depending on the fabric you choose, they will hang in a different way as well. Whereas the weight of furnishing fabric creates thick, neat folds, featherweight sheers behave in quite a different way. Soft sheer fabrics, such as voile and muslin, fall in thin, flat folds, which makes them ideal for a simple, unfussy decorative scheme. Sheers that have more body, such as organdy, organza, and linen fall into full rounded folds, lending a voluminous, almost dreamy quality to the overall look of a blind.

This page *The slightly stiff weave of organdy gives it plenty of body, which, combined with its intrinsic lightness, means it falls into voluptuous, rounded folds.*

Center *Feathers lend exquisite support to an otherwise plain blind. As well as their practical use, the feathers provide added visual interest.*

Right *The neat folds add an extra dimension to the blind and the fullness of the fabric catches the light and makes the blind appear luxurious.*

Added extras

Fastenings on clothes are very often used as embellishments. You can use buttons, buckles, snaps, and zippers in the same way on blinds to create smart details.

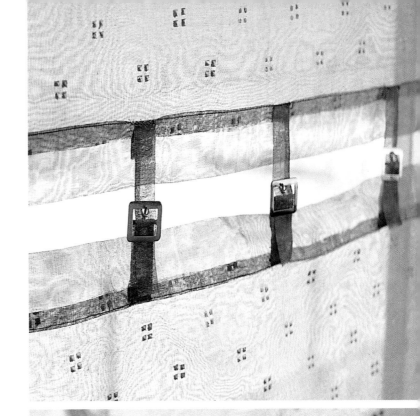

FASTENINGS CAN BE used to add fun and wit to simple blinds. They are most effective when they are given a more practical use rather than just being used as an embellishment. Here, buckles join two halves of a blind creating a play on light. Light can now stream between the two translucent sections, bringing extra brightness to the room without compromising on privacy. The metal buckles complement the metallic printed squares on the cotton organdy, which has been lined with translucent metal-shot organza. The lining has been brought to the front to make an elegant light-reflective border for a delicate feminine design.

Left *The neat, graphic quality of blinds offers plenty of scope for using witty treatments, such as these buckles. Using unusual fastenings like these allows you to bring your own personal touch to your blind.*

Right (top) *These metal buckles add charm while allowing extra light into the room.*

Right (bottom) *The metallic print on this organdy gives it a modern, yet pretty appearance.*

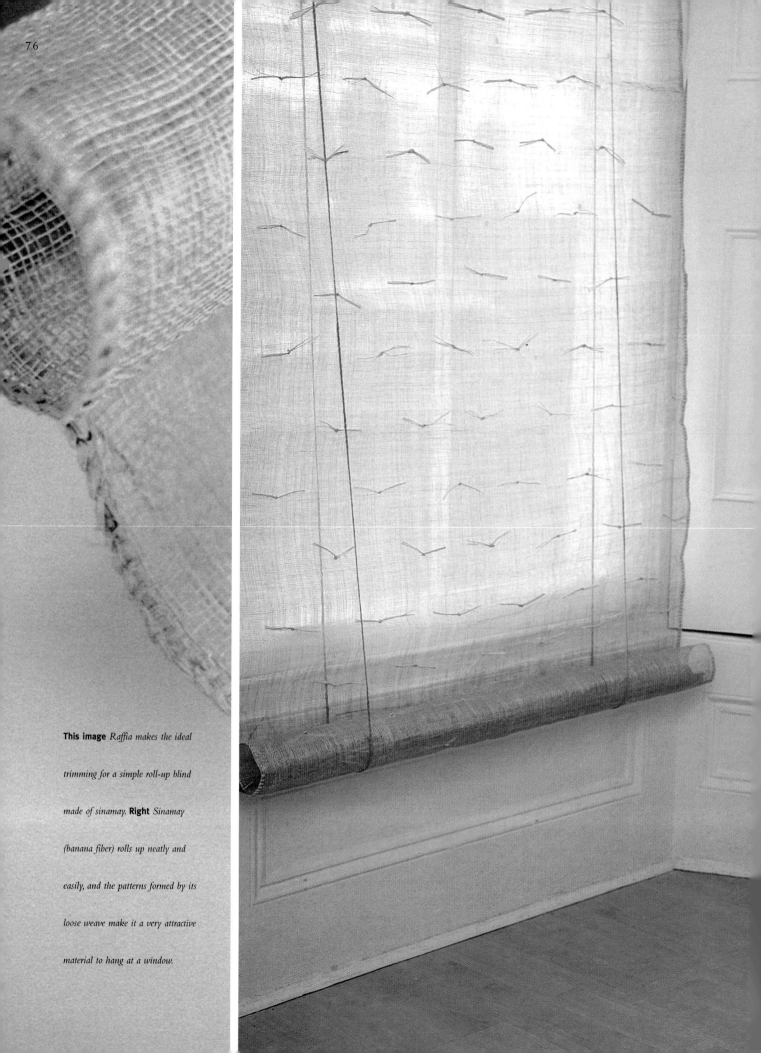

76

This image *Raffia makes the ideal trimming for a simple roll-up blind made of sinamay.* **Right** *Sinamay (banana fiber) rolls up neatly and easily, and the patterns formed by its loose weave make it a very attractive material to hang at a window.*

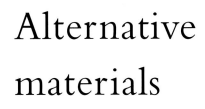

Alternative materials

Roll-up blinds are the simplest of all in construction and can be made in almost any material. This one is made from sinamay, used by milliners to trim hats.

THE DESIRE FOR increased natural light has created a market for roll-up blinds made from alternative materials such as split cane, paper, and micromesh. By looking for different, more unusual materials for your blinds, you can often devise your own inexpensive window treatments, which are truly individual in style. Sinamay, which is made of banana fiber and comes in a variety of colors is a glorious solution. Strong yet light filtering with plenty of body, it is easy to handle and also easy to hang. The loose weave of sinamay allows you to use strong, deep-toned colors, while still retaining a delicate sheer effect. The strength of the material makes it ideal for a more robust-looking treatment. For this blind, two layers of sinamay have been blanket-stitched together using raffia. Knotted raffia provides decoration for the body of the blind.

light

inside

Let the light through

In an ideal world all homes would be bathed throughout in sunlight. Unfortunately, this is rarely the case. Make the most of natural light by coaxing as much as you can into the darker parts of the house. A few simple tricks can really transform a gloomy room into something light and beautiful.

THE APPEAL OF loft-style living is the huge open space filled with light that can be sectioned off with translucent, or even transparent, room dividers. More traditional homes are already divided into rooms, corridors, and landings, all of which restrict the flow of light through the house. But there are ways to share the light around without resorting to major house alterations: using "borrowed light" and using "reflected light." When light is allowed from one area directly through to another, this is known as "borrowed light." Fan lights above the front door, typical of Georgian-style housing, are a prime example of this, letting light from the outside into gloomy entrance halls. You can adapt this idea inside the house, perhaps making a small window in an internal wall to bring natural light into a corridor or landing area. A less drastic variation is to replace door panels with glass, or even replace whole wooden doors with laminated safety glass. "Reflected light" is self-explanatory. Any mirror will brighten a room. Position the mirror opposite a window, or, in the case of a dark hallway, opposite an open door into a brighter room to make the most of ambient light. Many other surfaces are reflective: metal, glass, white-painted surfaces, and some fabrics. Stainless steel will brighten a gloomy kitchen, a white-painted garden wall opposite a window will reflect extra light into that room, and white cotton organdy will reflect and magnify any available light.

Left *This cupboard demonstrates both "borrowed" and "reflected light." Glass on three sides allows light to pass through the cupboard without casting shadows into the corners. The mirrored back reflects the light and magnifies it through the glass contents.*

Left *Light flooding into this room from windows along one wall is encouraged to pass from one space to another in several ways. Translucent panels in the sliding doors dividing one room from the other allow light through, even when the doors are closed. Beyond them, an open-plan living area means sitting and dining areas can share the same light. Floor-to-ceiling open shelves hardly inhibit the light, yet make a clear boundary between the two areas. By borrowing the light from where it streams in abundance, you can brighten those areas that need a little help to lighten up. Think of your home as a whole, rather than as a series of separate rooms, and try to imagine ways of using borrowed light. If some areas of your home are gloomy, furnish them with mirrors or translucent screens that reflect or let the light through from brighter areas of the house.*

Top *Bathrooms are often short of natural light. Here, the panels in this bathroom door have been fitted with sand-blasted glass panels. Although the glass offers full privacy, the translucency of the panels allows the bedroom and bathroom to share their light, each benefiting the other at different times of the day.*

Center *You can use furniture to create translucent room dividers. Even simple, freestanding, open bookshelves can provide a boundary between dining and living areas in a large room, without blocking out too much precious natural light.*

Bottom *Situated at the end of a long and gloomy corridor, the panels in this interior door have been replaced with glass so that the dining room and garden beyond can be glimpsed from the end of the passage-way. This allows valuable light to move between the areas, and turns the door into an attractive focal point.*

flexible

screening

transparent

space

light

ROOM DIVIDERS

concealing

filtering

Using room dividers

The key to successful open-plan living is a system of flexible, translucent room dividers that define the boundaries between two areas, and offer privacy, yet do not block out too much light.

THE ADVENT OF open-plan living has led to a demand for simple, imaginative ways to separate living spaces for different functions without cutting out the light. The most successful room dividers provide flexible solutions that can be adjusted with the changing requirements for the space. Classic folding screens, loved by the Victorians still offer an extremely useful, flexible form of room divider that can be moved around easily or folded up and put away when they are not required. Give them fresh modern appeal by fitting panels of translucent materials, such as translucent laminates, glass, Plexiglass sheets, strings of bead or shells, or even chicken wire or mesh, perhaps decorated with beads. You can use anything that is strong enough to work as a panel and that allows light to filter through.

For a more contemporary look, use ceiling-fixed room dividers made of light-diffusing translucent materials to separate the various areas of your room. The simplest way to do this is to install a pull-down blind that can be raised or lowered when needed. Alternatively, you can make up your own translucent panels to use as a room divider.

Choosing room dividers

Ceiling-hung dividers are well-suited to loft-style living. These translucent dividers give an updated feel to a traditional home.

THIS FABULOUS room divider is made up of feathers (pulled from a feather duster) sandwiched between sheets of tracing paper. These were then laminated. Hooked together in panels to reach ceiling height, it is easy to make one to fit your space. You can sandwich other translucent items between sheets of trace, such as skeletonized leaves, fine netting, or paper cutouts.

Alternatively, make the divider panels in plain tracing paper using just one color or several colors to create interesting patterns.

Right & far right *With each feather filling a panel, the overall look is modern and graphic.* **Center (top)** *Even the largest ostrich feathers are downy so light can filter through them.*

Center (bottom) *Each corner has been fitted with an eyelet to allow neat stainless steel hooks to link the panels.*

Simple screens

Opposite *Easily movable and fabulously flexible, screens are the traditional way to divide rooms or section off different areas within a room. They are ideal for today's multipurpose rooms, providing a discreet, yet light-giving way to divide a room. They can also provide extra privacy when used in front of the windows, as here. However, even using a classic framework, you can give a screen very different looks depending on what you use for the panels. Screens can be brought right up to date using a whole host of modern materials that complement the rest of the room's decorative scheme. Here, perforated aluminum has been used to give a traditional paneled screen a contemporary feel that looks wonderful with the fresh, striking colors used throughout the room. Perforated aluminum makes a brilliant panel material as it lets plenty of light through while offering privacy. It is available in a wide variety of styles with round, square, or diagonal piercings of various sizes offering you the choice of letting in more or less light, depending on your particular circumstances.*

Left *Perforated aluminum welcomes thousands of tiny shafts of light through from one area of the room to another. The shiny metallic surface reflects any ambient light back into the room, making it an ideal material to use in any room that has a tendency to be rather gloomy. The regular, geometric pattern of the pierced metal offers a structured alternative to the more usual, ethereal translucent materials. It brings a slightly more masculine appearance to a conventional screen and makes a bold design statement.*

Fretwork bedroom screens

Above and opposite *Intricate fretwork makes romantic, paneled bedroom screens*

that can also be used as window shutters, or to section off a washing or dressing area.

Wherever they are used, they let a joyous pattern of light through the pierced Indian-

inspired panels. The color-scheme is very calming and enhances the effect of the

natural light flooding into this tranquil bedroom. Imagine how cheering these delicate

patterns of sunlight would be when you wake in the morning. The beauty of these

screens is that they are so easy to adapt to suit your personal taste and fit in with the

decorative scheme of the room. Made of painted medium density fiberboard (MDF),

you can paint the screens to match the rest of the room, and then completely transform

them with a new coat of paint as the fancy takes you.

Screens for privacy

However much you desire light, there are times, even within the home, when privacy becomes the priority—such as in dressing areas, or to screen kitchen clutter from elegant dining areas.

WHERE THERE'S A need for areas of privacy, yet you still want light to flood your home, try using shutters. Using solid materials does not have to mean losing your precious daylight. Take a tip from eighteenth-century architects, who cut window shutters short to let the light in over the top even when they were shut. Short screens used as room dividers will have the same effect and can be opened wide or pushed together to admit the desired amount of light. Paint them in a pale or light-reflective finish to keep the light levels high. These reclaimed shutters have been given a new look with limed oak wood-treatment and decorative lines of clout nails that lend them a light reflective quality.

Left *A limed finish and orderly lines of nails give a totally new look to these reclaimed shutters. You can customize your screens to reflect the style of the rest of the room.*

Right *Reclaimed shutters can be used as screens or shutters, but need not block out all the light. Cut short, they allow the light to stream into the room over the top.*

Alternative materials

Left *Light positively dances through this glorious light-filled screen which is made of nothing more exotic than plastic wrap taped onto an acrylic frame, proving that even everyday items can be put to good decorative and practical use. All it takes is a little imagination. Made up of two outer "skins" with scrunched-up plastic wrap between, the screen is translucent rather than totally transparent. It also has a wonderful light-reflective quality as the light bounces off one skin and onto the other. The result is a screen that seems to be hardly there, yet also provides an efficient "veil" for privacy.*

Above *The curtain in front of the dress demonstrates the light-reflective quality of organdy as the sunlight behind the dress casts a shadow onto the delicate white fabric.*

Beaded curtain

Opposite   *Like raindrops on glass, the crystalline quality*

of this beaded curtain reflects the light, bringing brightness,

yet effectively dividing a room. Hung from the door frame

of the original dividing door, it accentuates the boundary

between the rooms, without shutting one off from the

other. The light sparkles on the beads just as if they were

chandelier droplets, but actually they are made of plastic.

But what does it matter? The effect is glorious and they

don't look out of place, even in a house that has real

antique chandeliers. They are light, unbreakable, and

inexpensive. Colored versions are also available for a more

wacky, modern effect. If you prefer to use real glass, you

could make your own bead curtain, using reasonably

priced Asian glass beads (though it would still be

more expensive to make than this ready-made version).

This page and far right   *Large droplets reflect plenty of*

light into the room, trapping the light the way raindrops

do on a sunny day. The droplets are arranged on strings

of sparkling beads to create a zig-zag pattern.

romantic

dreamy

TRANSLUCENT

ethereal

secrecy

intimate

privacy

fresh

FURNISHINGS

Choosing furnishings

Gossamer-fine sheers, used as canopies or to enclose parts of a room, have a similar effect to room dividers. However, as they are softer and more fluid, they evoke a more veiled romantic feel.

LIKE ROOM DIVIDERS, translucent furnishings help to create a feeling of lightness and airiness throughout the house, and, through their ethereal appearance, often create a feeling of an extra dimension as well. The trick is to keep the dividers simple. Even a basic panel of fabric, hung from a curtain rail mounted to the ceiling, can be an effective space-saving room divider, perfect for open-plan living from a state-of-the-art, modern loft to a tiny bedroom/sitting room. The idea is to screen off one area from another without cutting out the light or using up too much precious space. This is a fast and easy way to screen off a relaxing dining area from a less-than-immaculate kitchen space or a cluttered office corner from the main living area.

For a simple room divider that you can make in an evening from a length of fabric, make a bottom hem deep enough for a slim dowel to weight the fabric down, add a tab-top tie heading to fix to the rail, and leave the selvage untouched.

Translucent panels also make delightful canopies that create an intimate, romantic atmosphere, while also creating a feeling of space and light throughout the room.

Left *A length of fabric hanging from the ceiling makes a simple, but extremely effective room divider. The fabric gives the dining area an intimate atmosphere. It divides the two areas while allowing the whole room to be used when required. Made of sheer linen, it is light-reflective while it also veils the area beyond.*

Layered room divider

Opposite *Sliding glass doors between a living room and patio offer an open vista and the feeling of one-room living. A curtain hung at the door has the effect of a room divider and can be drawn or opened to offer a flexible style of living. To link the rich jewel colors of the furniture with the white walls, the divider was designed using a combination of emerald green cotton and white cotton voile with a fine green window check. The divider was made in layers to give it extra body, and so that extra flashes of green showed through when the delicate fabric billowed in the breeze.*

Far left (top) *The combination of box pleats, window checks, and soft floaty layers make a smart, yet feminine room divider. By using the basically white voile as the main fabric, the divider retains a light and airy feel.*

Far left (bottom) *The box pleats are sewn down to the bottom of the second square to keep the divider looking neat and tidy. For the rest of the length of the divider, the top layers are free to move around in the breeze and give the whole room a light, floaty look.*

Canopies

Even just a whisper of voile adds a sense of romance to any bed, but if you want a fresh, light-filtered look, keep sheer canopies simple, using them in flat panels.

Gossamer-fine voile draped over a four poster bed appears to filter the light, creating a wonderful sense of mystery and adding to the importance of the bed within the room. As most homes now have central heating, heavily gathered curtains are no longer needed to keep out drafts, so drapes can be enjoyed for their sheer beauty. We can now choose the fabrics we love without practical considerations. Simple panels offer a sense of lightness and airiness, and if they don't cover the full width of the bed, the effect is even lighter. It couldn't be simpler to hang a piece of fabric the length of the bed and allow it to drape over the front and back to achieve a delightful, romantic look.

Right *Aqua check voile used to drape this bed brings a welcome splash of color without overpowering an otherwise white room. By adding a fringe trimming to the front edge, the drape takes on a finished look. Using sheer fabrics is a wonderful way to create a dreamy, fairy tale of a bedroom, while retaining a simple, uncluttered look.*

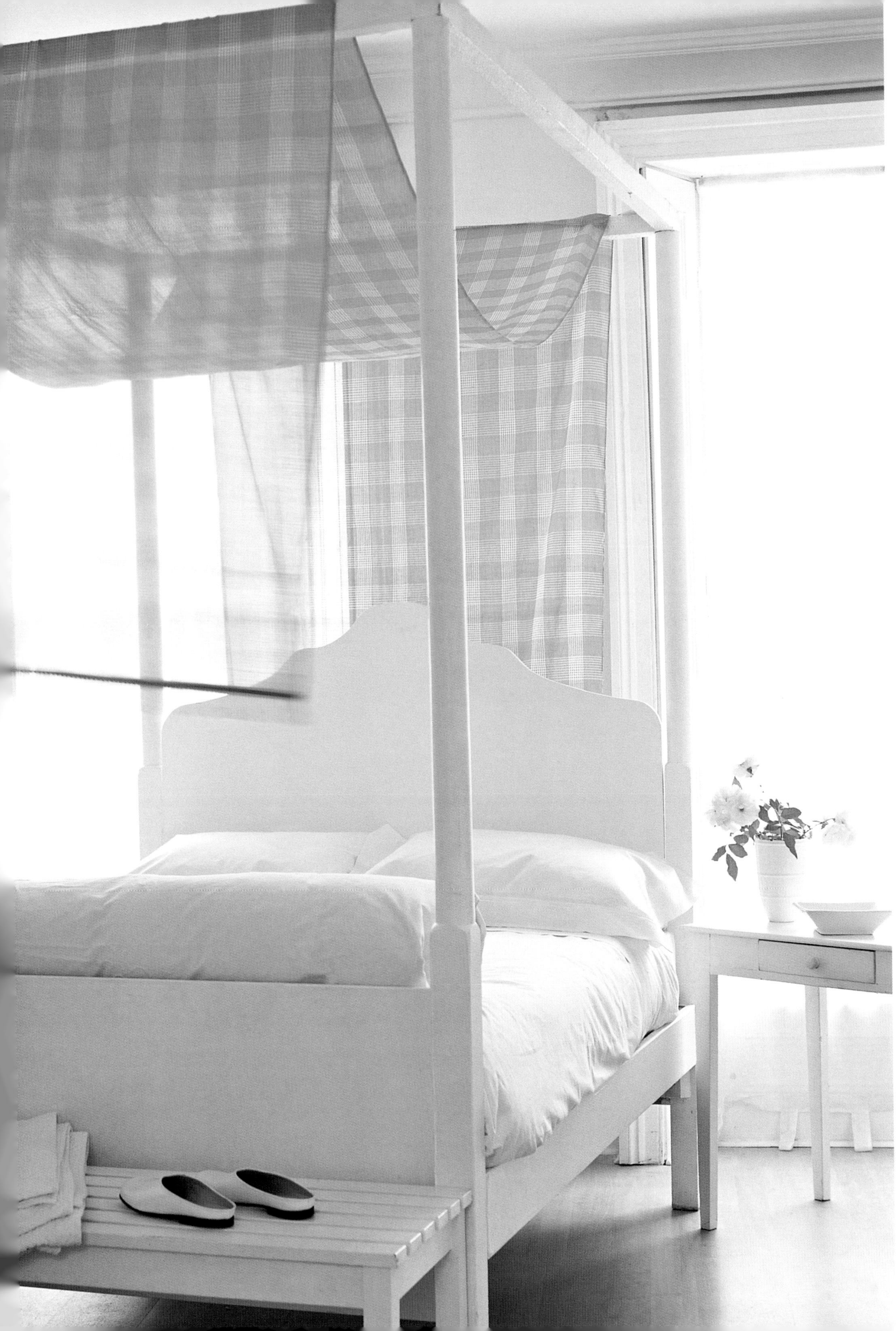

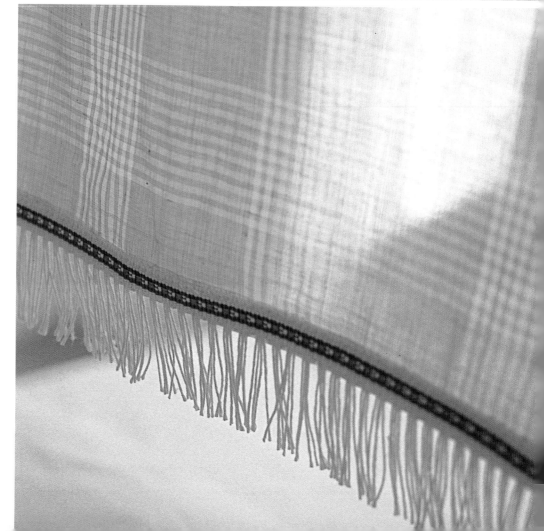

Left & Center (bottom)

You only need about 40 in.

(1 m) of trimming to finish off one

width of fabric, so why not buy the

very best quality trimming?

Center (top) *The drapes have been*

hung like curtain panels at the back

and sides of the bed for a smart look.

A plain white organdy panel looks

ethereal at the foot of the bed.

Far right *Mosquito nets make*

delightful canopies.

& practice

Measuring, cutting, & stitching

Important notes

1 For practical reasons, the conversions of metric into imperial measurements are not exact—choose one or the other and stick to it for measuring, cutting, and making.

2 Since sheers are very fine fabrics, the seam allowances are smaller than for furnishing fabrics. If you wish to adapt any instructions for use with furnishing fabrics, double the seam allowances.

Measuring

Accurate measurements are the key to successful window treatments and you really cannot check them too carefully. It is a good idea to measure everything three times—just like carpentry students are told to do. It's also a good idea to ask someone to help you measure, as a tape held firmly at both ends will give you a more accurate result and you can check with each other as you go along.

Where to measure

Curtains can be hung from one of three places: above the window molding, on a flat part of the molding, or within the recess if the window is recessed. Blinds can be hung from either of the last two options. Decide which option you want before beginning to measure. You will also need to decide whether the curtain

or blind will be hung to the window sill or to the floor.

How to measure

You will need a steel ruler, which is more accurate than a cloth tape. Try to be methodical. For example, you may always wish to write the width before the length so you don't confuse the measurements. Decide whether you want to use metric or imperial measurements and stick to them. If you're measuring for a new house that you haven't yet moved into, take a photograph of the window and take all the measurements so that you can decide at leisure where you want to affix the curtains or blinds. Draw a sketch of the window with arrows, and show where the measurement finishes using stop lines. Then write the measurement along the arrow. When you have measured all the dimensions, go back to the beginning again and recheck them.

Measuring for curtains that hang from above the molding (1)

These are usually hung from a rail about 4 in. (10 cm) above the molding, although they can be hung higher if the ceiling height allows. The bracket for the rail is usually about 2 in. (5 cm) out from the molding with the finials projecting out from that. Measure from the curtain rail to the sill or floor for the length, and the length of the curtain rod between the finials for the width.

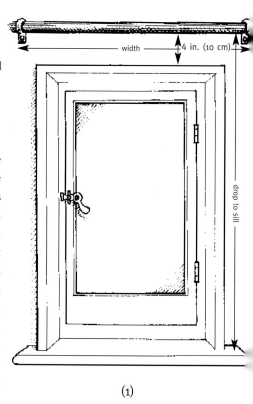

(1)

Measuring for curtains or blinds that hang from the molding (2)

Moldings can be wide or narrow: modern ones are often flat, although older houses can have moldings that have outer and inner edges. Blinds sit best if their supports are affixed to the flat middle part of the molding. Curtain rods can be affixed to the outside edge of the molding if there is enough space for a firm attachment. Measure the length from the top of the affixing batten, curtain rod, or rail, to the window sill, or to the floor if preferred. The width for blinds should be from the outside edge of the flat part of the molding; curtains should be the width of the curtain rod.

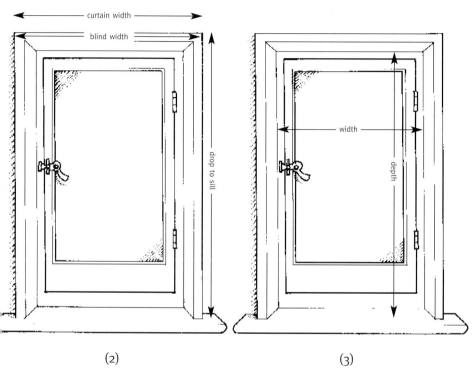

(2)   (3)

Measuring for curtains or blinds fitted within a recess (3)

Measure the full width of the recess to find the finished width of your curtain. Measure the length from the top of the recess, down to the sill.

Estimating fabric for banner curtains

The measurements for the windows will give you the finished width of your curtain or blind. Traditionally, this is the width of the gathered or pleated curtain at the window. However, all the curtains in this book are ungathered banners, designed to create an uncluttered look.

These curtains are beautifully simple to look at and to make. None of the curtains featured in this book uses gathering tape, so there are no complicated multiples for you to work out. However, it is still better to be generous when you are buying your fabric. Allow an extra 2 in. (5 cm) either side for curtains, for movement. You also need a further ¾ in. (2 cm) either side for side hems and ¾ in. (2 cm) either side for each seam you are going to join. This will give you the width that you need to cut. Work out how many widths of fabric you will need to cover the window, and then multiply this by the length of the drop, which is length of the finished curtains with an extra 4 in. (10 cm) for top and bottom turnings. This will give you the cut length for your fabric.

Estimating fabric for sheer blinds

Blinds should fit exactly if they are to hang properly. Add ⅜ in. (1 cm) either side plus ⅜ in. (1 cm) either side for any seaming to find the cut width. Multiply this by the drop, which is the finished length of the blind plus 4 in. (10 cm) for top and bottom hems.

Cutting and preparing sheer fabric

The most important thing is to make sure that you always start with a straight edge by pulling out a thread at the raw edge, across the fabric from selvage to selvage. The space it leaves between its two neighbors will give you a straight line to cut along. Measure down the length of the first drop, pull another thread and cut along that space. Carry on like this until you have cut out all the drops required. Sometimes, you may need to join part widths together. Plan out how you are going to do this before you start cutting. For example, if you are making a blind that needs to be more than one width of fabric wide, you may wish to have a full width in the center with narrower widths either side. If you are making a pair of curtains that requires three drops of fabric, make each curtain with a full drop at the inside edge and half a drop on the outside edge. Keep the cut widths straight by measuring in from the selvage at several points, marking the point with a pin and then carefully cutting along the pin line.

Stitching sheer fabrics

Sheer fabric is usually fine, loosely woven, and slippery to handle. It frays and snags easily, so it needs to be treated with special care. Its translucency also means that all your workings will show, so you cannot allow the wrong side of the fabric to look messy. Fortunately, sheers crease neatly into tiny turnings and seams.

Making French seams (1)

The most efficient and neat way to deal with sheers is to make tiny French seams. These look good from both sides and also prevent the fabric from fraying. Place the fabric lengths wrong-sides together, stitch a ⅜ in. (1 cm) seam as close to the edge of the fabric as possible, trim to ⅛ in. (3 mm) and press open. Turn the fabric right-sides together along the seam line and stitch a seam through two layers of fabric. This captures the raw edges within the seam.

Machine fell seams (jean seams) (2)

This is a robust way of making a feature of seams. With right-sides together stitch a ⅝ in. (1.5 cm) seam. Trim one allowance by ¼ in. (0.5 cm) so that you have one side of the seam wider than the other. Turn in the edge of the wider seam allowance and topstitch over the trimmed allowance. On the finished seam, the right-side of the fabric appears to have two lines of parallel stitching, and the wrong side looks like a flat seam parallel to a line of stitching. This seam is popular on sportswear.

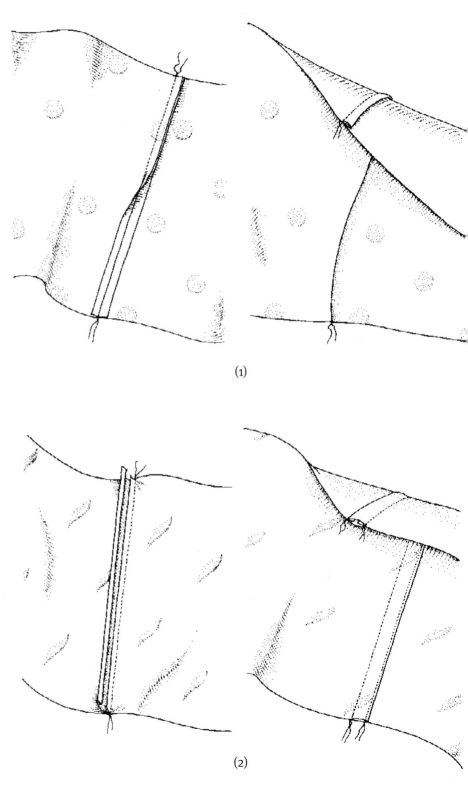

(1)

(2)

The projects

Limed oak shutters
(see page 94)

Reclaimed shutters take on a refreshingly modern look when given a limed finish and decorated with builders' clout nails. In Georgian times, shutters were fitted short of the window's top to allow extra light into the room over the shutter while protecting the privacy of the house. This makes finding reclaimed shutters to fit your windows a less difficult task: choose shutters that are tall enough to protect your privacy, and either the exact width of your window or a little wider.

Materials

Pair of reclaimed shutters

Limed oak woodwash

Paintbrush

Pencil

Awl

Clout nails with ⅛ in. (3 mm) heads (about 1000 for a pair of shutters 6 ft. 6 in. / 2 m high)

Hammer

1   *Have the shutters dipped professionally to strip off the old paint and varnish finishes.*
2   *Ask a carpenter to plane the shutters to fit the width of the opening.*
3   *Brush the shutters with a translucent finish. These were brushed with two coats of a proprietary limed oak woodwash.*
4   *Lay the shutters flat on the floor. Using a pencil, mark out the desired positions of the clout nails. The positions will depend on the size and design of the shutters.*
5   *Make guide holes using the awl.*
6   *Hammer the nails into position.*
7   *Using hinges, affix the shutters to the windows.*

2

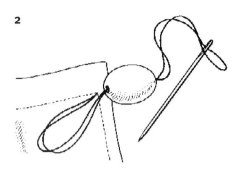

3

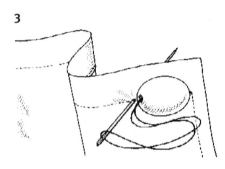

4

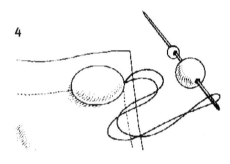

5

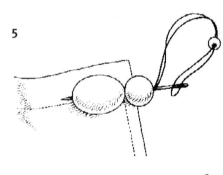

6

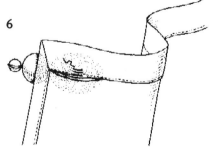

Beaded additions

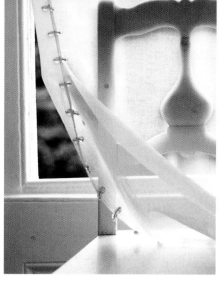

Beaded additions
(see page 32)

Lend sparkle to a pair of ready-made pure-white organdy curtains using pretty, translucent glass beads. Bold beads make a real statement hung at a window, although they need to be sewn on firmly to make sure their weight does not pull them off when the curtains are in use.

Materials

A ready-made organdy curtain or enough organdy to make your own. Enough beads to space about 1 ½ in. (4 cm) apart down each side of each curtain. Three types of clear Indian glass beads were used for these curtains: Flat oval ¾ in. (2 cm) long round, round ⅜ in. (1 cm) diameter and small round ⅛ in. (0.3 cm) Strong polyester thread from bead suppliers Needle

1   *Measure the side of the finished curtain and work out the spacing. It's easier to use an equivalent measurement, rather than an actual measurement. That way, there's no need for a ruler or tape. For this curtain, the measurement was the width of the first two fingers.*
2   *Use the oval bead as an "anchor." Place it near the edge of the curtain so that the hole at the end lines up with the line of stitching down the edge of the curtain.*
3   *Make a large knot in double thread. Pass the needle from the back at the stitching line. Thread on the bead, pass the needle down*

through the fabric at the other end and up to the right-side of the stitching line again.
4   *Thread on the large round bead and then the small round bead.*
5   *Pass the thread over the tiny bead, then back again through the two larger beads and down to the underside again.*
6   *Finish off with three tiny stitches at the middle of the back of the oval bead. It is important that you finish off here: if you finish off near the end of the bead, its weight will pull the threads loose and the beads will eventually come off.*

Leaf-bead edging
(see page 36)

A floaty, feminine printed cotton voile curtain is given added visual interest by the addition of an edging of glass beads. This project uses similar techniques to Beaded additions (left).

Materials

Curtains in printed cotton voile
Japanese glass lamp beads on brass wire loops—either clear glass or frosted, or alternating (as used here)
Tiny frosted glass florets
Vial of seed beads
Needle and thread

1   *Firmly stitch on one leaf bead. Position it so that the leaf is pointing outwards from the edge of the curtain.*
2   *Next, thread on a frosted glass floret and a seed bead.*
3   *Pass the thread over the seed bead, back through the floret and the leaf bead to the back of the work and finish off firmly.*

1

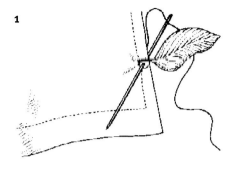

2

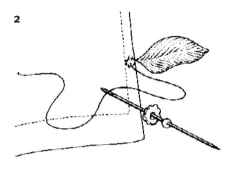

3

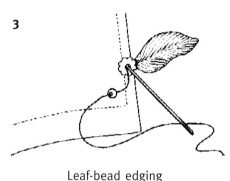

Leaf-bead edging

Clever paneling
(see page 38)

Hand-painted organza teamed with a plain organza makes an attractive, yet elegant window panel with a difference. The plain organza is cut to the full width of the window and a printed panel stitched on top to make a central panel of double thickness. The finished piece is simply clipped into position on a yachting wire using curtain clips. There is no need to use complicated headings, so this curtain is beautifully simple to make.

Materials
Enough plain metal-shot organza to make a full-width banner for the window
Enough painted metal-shot organza to create a central banner the full length of the window
Gold thread
Curtain clips

1 *Cut the plain organza to the full width of the window plus ¾ in. (2 cm) either side and the full length of the window plus an extra ¾ in. (2 cm) top and bottom.*
2 *Cut some full-length painted organza to make a central panel of pleasing proportion. You can decide for yourself how wide you would like the central panel to be. Your decision will be based on the nature of the pattern on the painted organza and the finished effect that you want to achieve*
3 *Press in a ⅜ in. (2 cm) single turning to the back along the long edges of the printed organza, then turn and press in a ⅜ in. (2 cm) double hem along the long sides of the plain organza.*
4 *Fold both pieces of fabric in half lengthways and mark with pins at intervals to find the center. Lie the plain organza face up on a flat surface. Lay the painted organza face up on top of it. Line up the pins and work a line*

of tacking along them. Smooth the fabric out from the middle and run another line of tacking halfway between the central line and the edges of the painted voile, then another near the turnings. Repeat on the other side.
5 *Using the gold thread, stitch down one edge of the turned-in painted voile. Work another line of top-stitching just inside the first. Repeat on the other side.*
6 *In the same way, neatly work a double line of gold top-stitching at the finished edges of the curtain.*
7 *Press in a ¾ in. (2 cm) double hem to the back along the top and bottom edges.*
8 *Work a double row of gold top-stitching top and bottom.*

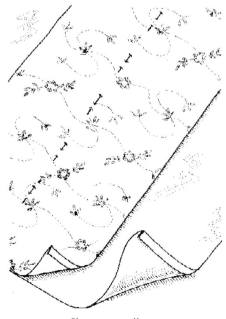

Clever paneling

4

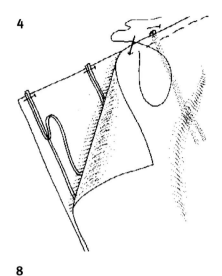

8

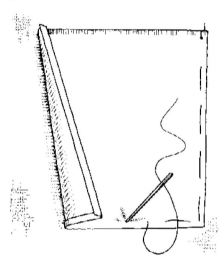

9

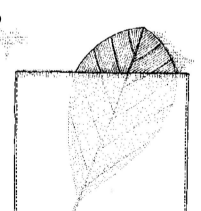

Magnolia curtain

Magnolia curtain

(see page 50)

This delightful, tie-top curtain is made in cotton organdy, appliquéd with pockets for skeletonized magnolia leaf. You can choose how many pockets you want and where to place them on the curtain.

Materials

Enough pure cotton organdy to make 2 ½ times the length of the finished size of the curtain, allowing for ⅜ in. (1 cm) turnings all round

Matching thread

Selection of skeletonized magnolia leaves

1 *Cut the curtain to the finished size, adding an extra ¾ in. (2 cm) to the length and ¾ in. (2 cm) to the width to give ⅜ in. (2 cm) all round for turnings. Cut another piece to match. Lay this on a flat surface and lay the magnolia leaves on top to make a pleasing design.*

2 *Measure out the sizes of the pockets to accommodate them. Cut the pockets so the selvages make up the top open end, and allow ¼ in. (0.5 cm) for turnings at the raw edges. Work out how many ties you need—you will need a pair at intervals of about 8 in. (20 cm), then cut each one about 12 in. (30 cm) long and ¾ in. (2 cm) wide.*

3 *Make the ties by pressing in tiny hems along the long edges, then folding them wrong-sides together in half lengthways. Top stitch along the open long edge.*

4 *Lie one cut curtain piece right-side down on a flat surface. Pin the pairs of ties in position with the raw ends lined up with the raw edges of the top of the curtain. Place the other curtain piece right-side up on top and baste the two pieces together.*

5 *Stitch along the top edge, down one side, along the bottom edge and halfway up one side, making ⅜ in. (1 cm) seams. Trim the seams and press open.*

6 *Turn the curtain through to the right-side and press flat, turning in the open edges.*

7 *Slip-stitch the open edges together.*

8 *On the pockets, turn in and press ¼ in. (0.5 cm) and baste into position on the curtain with the selvage to the top and top-stitch around the turned-in edges.*

9 *Slip the magnolia leaves into the pockets.*

10 *Tie the finished curtain into position. Use a simple method of hanging, such as these wrought iron nails, to support the curtain.*

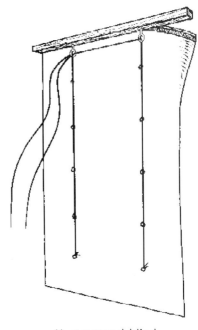

Unstructured blind

Unstructured blind
(see page 66)

This blind makes a very pretty, unfussy sheer window treatment. An unstructured blind is very similar to a Roman blind, except it does not have rigid supports, so as it pulls up, it folds into gentle cascades rather than neat ridges. You need to make it 1½ times the length of the window measurement so that it creates fullness as it pulls up. Since you can see through sheer blinds, this one makes a feature of the cords, which were made from organdy ribbon, rather than cord.

Materials

Main fabric in metal-shot organdy

Lining layer in white cotton organdy

Organdy ribbon—allow twice the sum of the length, plus the width of the blind for each ribbon pull cord.

Enough small white plastic rings to allow one per every 12 in. (30 cm) of the length of the blind multiplied by the number of cords.

A batten the width of the blind, painted, if you like, and the necessary affixatives.

Stick and Sew touch-and-close fastening the width of the blind.

Thread

Cleat and affixatives

1 *Affix the batten to the desired position on the window frame or reveal. Affix the cleat to the right-hand molding.*

2 *Cut the fabric to the width of the finished blind plus ¾ in. (2 cm) for turnings and 1½ times the length of the blind—both in the top fabric and the lining fabric.*

3 *Turn in and press a ⅜ in. (2 cm) hem at the top edge of both pieces of fabric.*

4 *Lay the lining fabric right-side up on a flat surface and the main fabric right-side down on top of the lining fabric.*

5 *Pin, baste and stitch ⅜ in. (2 cm) seams around the sides and bottom of the blind. Trim the seams and press open.*

6 *Turn through to the right-side.*

7 *Turn in the top edges and baste to close. Pin and baste the "sew" part of the fastening to the top of the blind through two layers.*

8 *Stick the "stick" layer of the touch-and-close fastening to the batten at the window.*

9 *Measure 12 in. (30 cm) up from the*

bottom of the blind and mark the cord positions. These should either be marking the blind into thirds, or fifths, depending on the width. Sew on a small ring at these points. Continue measuring and marking approximately every 12 in. (30 cm) or similar multiple, to give even spacing for the rings up the length of the blind. Sew the rings into position.

10 *Affix the screw eyes into the underside of the batten at exactly the position of the ribbon pulls.*

11 *Tie a length of ribbon to each bottom ring, then thread the ribbon up through the rings to the top of the blind.*

12 *Use the touch-and-close fastening to hold the blind in position, then thread the left-hand ribbon through the left-hand screw eye and then through any screw eyes along the length of the blind until it reaches the right-hand screw eye.*

13 *Thread the next ribbon up through the rings, through its corresponding screw eyes and along to the right screw eye, until all the ribbons are threaded through to the right.*

14 *Bring the ribbons down together to the cleat, and wind around the cleat to secure them in place. The blind is now ready for use.*

Roman blind with metallic stay supports

(see page 70)

Roman blinds are a classic, elegant treatment that can work really well in sheer fabrics. You can make them in the traditional way using battens, or, since the fabric is translucent, you may wish to use alternative supports that are beautiful in themselves. This blind simply substitutes metallic stays for the battens. Usually used in corsets or other garments, these can be bought at the desired length from fine fabric stores. These white cotton organdy blinds are self-lined, so calculate the cut width and then double it for the fabric requirements.

Materials

White cotton organdy

Stick-and-Sew touch-and-close fastening the width of the blind

A batten the width of the blind, plus screws to affix it to the window frame

Metallic supports—you'll need one every 12 in. (30 cm) plus one extra. Allow for the width of the fabric multiplied by the amount of supports.

Metallic grosgrain ribbon about ⅜ in. (1 cm) wide to use as cord. You'll need to allow for one cord per 10 in. (25 cm) of the width of the

blind, each the sum of twice the length, plus the width of the blind

Small plastic rings—allow one every 12 in. (30 cm) of the length of the blind, multiplied by the number of cords.

Screw eyes—one for each cord

One cleat

Dressmaker's wax pencil

1 *Cut the finished width of organdy, plus turnings of ⅜ in. (1 cm) either side, and double the length plus ¼ in. (2 cm) for turnings. Leave the selvage on at least one side, then press in a ¼ in. (0.5 cm) turning along that edge.*

2 *With right-sides together, fold the fabric in half widthways. Pin and baste. Sew a narrow seam of ¼ in. (0.5 cm) along the top of the blind and down one side, leaving the pressed-in selvage open. Remove the basting, turn to the right-side and press.*

3 *Work out the positions of the supports. These are best between 8–12 in. (20–30 cm)*

apart, the bottom one needs to be a half-fold and the top one at least 14 in. (35 cm) from the top. It is best to have an odd number of struts. Roughly estimate the number and spacing of struts, then draw it out to scale on a piece of paper to make sure the plan works.

4 *Lay the blind right-side down on a flat surface. Start at the bottom and measure up half a space and mark with wax pencil at several places along the blind's width. Then, using a steel ruler, make a wax-pencil line along the full width. Draw another line above this, leaving enough space to slip in the supports.*

5 *Measure a full space up from the top line. Using wax pencil, mark and draw in the stitch lines for the next support. Continue until about 14 in. (35 cm) from the top.*

6 *Cut the support strip to the blind width. Stitch the bottom line of support casing. Slip in the support, tucking it against the sewn seam at one side of the blind and under the turned-in hem of the top layer of the blind.*

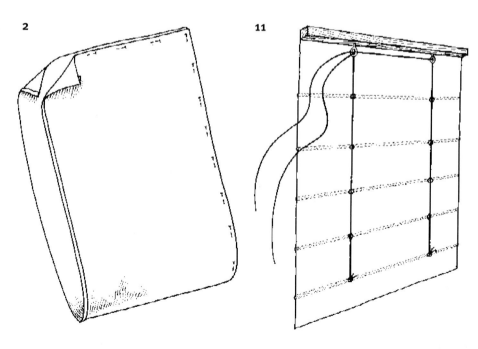

Roman blind with metallic stay supports

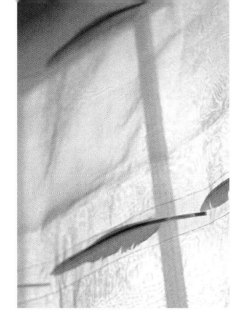

Using a zipper foot, stitch the top line of the casing. Repeat for the other supports.

7 *At the top edge of the blind, slip a final support strip into the front of the blind. This last support will be used as a trim only. Baste the soft side of the touch-and-close fastening to the back of the blind. Stitch into position. The stitch lines securing the touch-and-close fastening will become the casing for the final support strip.*

8 *Next decide where on the blind you would like the cords to be. Measure in from the edge and firmly stitch a ring into position behind the lowest support. Take the same measurement in from the edge of the next support and repeat all the way up the blind. Repeat with the other cord positions.*

9 *Place the batten to the window frame. When you are happy with the position, affix the batten firmly into position. Stick the hook side of the touch-and-close fastening to the front surface of the batten.*

10 *Tie a length of ribbon to each of the bottom rings and thread up through the rings. Fasten the blind into position.*

11 *Using a pencil, carefully mark the positions of the cords on the underside of the batten. Next, affix in a screw eye in each of the marked positions. Thread the ribbon through these screw eyes, passing all the pieces through to one side of the blind.*

12 *Affix the cleat to the side of the window frame where the ribbons have come out and wind the ribbons round to secure in place. The blind is now ready for use.*

Feather support blind
(see page 72)

This was made in the same way as the Roman blind, but white swans' quills were substituted for the metallic stays. This obviously means that you need to stitch wider channels for this blind.

Buckle blind
(see page 74)

Cotton organdy printed with a tiny motif has been complemented by a lining and border of toning metal-shot organza. The buckles continue the metal theme. Here, they have been used to join two sections of the same blind, giving the effect of a pierced material, rather than a diffused blind.

Materials
Metal-shot organza
Printed cotton organdy to the finished width minus 2⅜ in. (6 cm) and the finished length minus 2⅜ in. (6 cm)
Small metal buckles—allow approximately one every 6 in. (15 cm)
Metal eyelets and eyelet tool
Thread

1 *Cut the metal-shot organza to the finished width plus 4 in. (10 cm) and the finished length plus 4 in. (10 cm).*

2 *Fold the printed organdy in half widthways, mark and cut to form the two sections of the blind. Repeat with the metal-shot organza.*

3 *Make sure the edges of the organza are exactly square. Do this by pulling a thread near the very edge of each of the eight edges and cutting along the gaps they leave. This is important if you are to make neat and accurate miters.*

4 *Lay one piece of metal-shot organza right-side down on a flat surface. Lay one piece of printed cotton organdy right-side up on top of this. Make sure it is lying centrally by measuring out from all edges at several places to check it is a constant measurement. Pin, then baste down the center vertically and horizontally to secure the position. If the blind is large, run several more lines of basting to make sure that it stays flat. Then repeat with the other two pieces to make the second section of the blind.*

5 *Measure in 2 in. (5 cm) from the edge of the metal-shot organza in several places on all sides and mark. Press the organza forward along this line to form the border. Press in the raw edge by ⅜ in. (1 cm) all round.*

6 *Unfold the folded edges, then fold in the corner diagonally so that all the previous creases line up. Now cut off the corner, leaving an allowance of ⅜ in. (1 cm). Now fold the bottom edge up. Turn in the seam allowance on the adjoining side edge, fold the side over and make a neat line of stitching along the diagonal. Repeat on the other seven corners.*

7 *Top-stitch around the inside edge of the metal-shot organza.*

8 *To prepare the buckle straps, cut two pieces of metal-shot organza for each buckle 1½ in. (4 cm) wide and 4¾ in. (12 cm) long. With right-sides together, fold them in half lengthways and stitch. Turn to right-side and press. The buckles go on the bottom piece of the* *blind with the prong pointing upwards. Fold one strap in half widthways and make a small hole in the center for the prong. Bring the two ends down, fold the ends inwards and hand-stitch to the bottom right-hand corner of the blind, following the line of stitching made to create a border with the metal-shot organza. Repeat on the left-hand side and at equal distances along the width of the blind.*

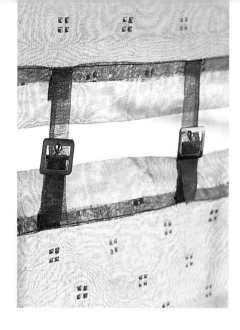

4

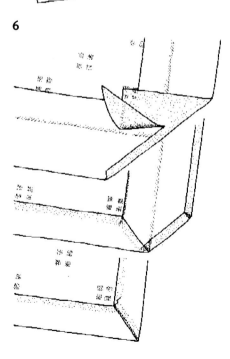

6

Buckle blind

9 *The other straps go on the top part of the blind. Turn in and slip-stitch the raw ends at one end and turn in and stitch the other end to the corresponding parts of the blind to the buckles. Using an eyelet tool, affix one eyelet into each strap just above the top edge of the blind. Buckle the two parts together.*

10 *Make hanging loops from lengths of metal-shot organza measuring ¾ in. (2 cm) by 4 in. (10 cm). Use the same method that you used for preparing the buckle straps, then fold in half and neatly sew one each to the top corners of the blind.*

9

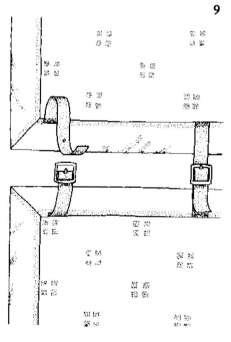

Sinamay roll-up blind (8)
(see page 76)

Sinamay is an extremely versatile material made from banana fiber. It is available in a wide variety of colors, and it can be made up into very effective and unusual sheer window treatments.

Materials

Sinamay

⅜ in. (1 cm) dowel the width of the blind

Paint to match sinamay

1 in. (2.5 cm) wooden batten

Screws to affix batten

Natural raffia

Tapestry needle

20 in. (50 cm) of webbing tape about ¾ in. (2 cm) wide to match the sinamay

4 small brass rings

Staple gun

2 brass round-head screws

Fine braided jute cording

1 *Cut the dowel and the batten to the desired width. Paint and allow to dry.*

2 *Cut the sinamay to the finished width and twice the finished length plus ¾ in. (2 cm). Fold it in half widthways to give a double layer. Place one piece of dowel in the fold and pin the two layers of sinamay together near the dowel end. Using natural raffia, blanket-stitch up one side of the blind to join the two layers and then stitch up from the bottom on the other side. Turn in the raw top edges of sinamay and blanket-stitch together.*

3 *Run a neat line of running stitches in raffia across the width of the blind, holding the bottom dowel in position.*

4 *Decorate the surface of the blind by making individual stitches in raffia, knotting them together and trimming the ends. You can choose where to place the stitches. This design was done in rows one hand's width apart.*

5 *Cut the webbing into two equal pieces and fold in half. Slip two brass rings on each piece, then make strong French seams to join the ends together.*

6 *Using a staple gun, affix the blind to the top edge of the batten, then place the two webbing loops with a brass ring to the back and a brass ring to the front centrally over the top about 6 in. (15 cm) from each edge. Staple the loops and rings into position.*

7 *Next, lift the blind up and use the screws to attach the batten to the molding. These stays should not show once the blind is hanging in position.*

8 *Cut the cord in half. Tie one piece to each brass ring at the back of the blind. Let them run down the back of the blind, up the front and through the brass rings at the front. Bring the cords to one side and affix the cleat in the molding at that side. Roll up the blind by hand in the first instance and take up the slack in the cords. The weight of the dowel will now allow the blind to run freely when the cords are tightened or loosened.*

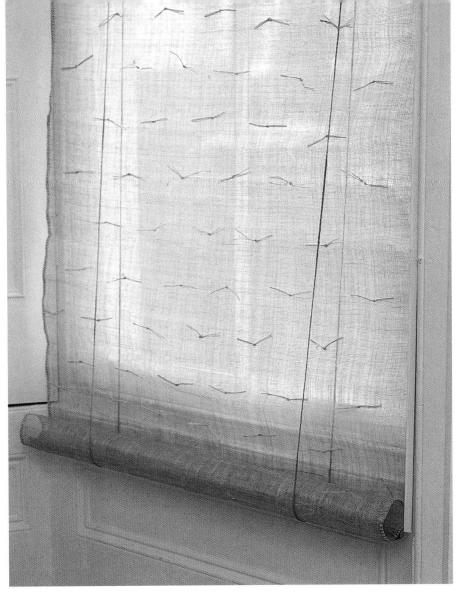

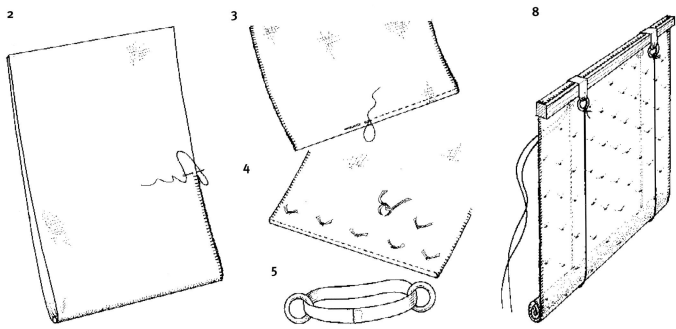

Sinamay blind

Layered fabric divider

(see page 104)

Soft floaty voile takes on a modern, tailored look with a layered design inspired by inverted box pleats. It is made in two layers so that color from the underlayer can be seen glimpsed through the top layer of checked panels. This layered effect also lends extra body to the voile. This design works well with checks because it's neat, and because you can use the lines as pleating guides.

Materials

Four widths of the main fabric multiplied by the length of the drop

One width of the contrast multiplied by the length of the drop

Eyelets and eyelet tool

Thread

1 *First work out the underlayer, which is window-checked voile alternated with emerald green. Since each treatment is custom-made, and fabrics can vary, experiment with your fabrics to find what suits your situation and your personal taste. You can use this room divider for inspiration. Here, the emerald voile was cut into four equal sections, then alternated with window-check sections—three whole checks with half a check each side—to make best use of the fabric and to complement the fabric's design. So, for each of the two curtains, there is a central checked piece, flanked by solid green strips, and then checked pieces for the outside drops. These were stitched together using French seams.*

2 *Turn in and stitch the sides and a 2 in. (5 cm) hem at the bottom.*

3 *The top layer is loose panels of checked fabric, each turned in at the sides to meet in the middle of the green strips. Cut three strips for each curtain, each the width of the sum of a checked strip plus a green strip. Turn in and stitch each of the long lengths and make a 2 in. (5 cm) hem at the bottom.*

4 *Find the center of each green strip and mark it with a pin.*

4 *Working from the center of the central panel of one curtain, line up the top layer checks with the underlayer checks and pin into position. At the center of the green strip, turn the check panel under and pin. Continue with the other panels. Baste all along the top.*

5 *Turn in ¾ in. (2 cm) at the top edges. Pin and baste. Stitch close to the top and then again ¾ in. (2 cm) further down.*

6 *Make a vertical line of stitching 8 in. (20 cm) down each side of each pleat.*

7 *Affix one eyelet at the top edge where the pleats meet in the center of the green strips.*

1

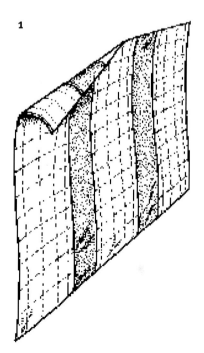

4

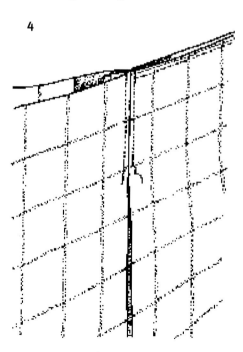

5

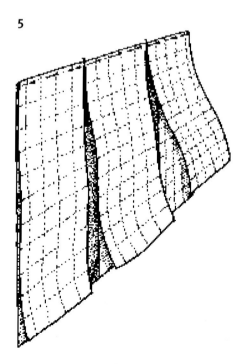

Layered fabric divider

Feather room divider
(see page 88)

This divider can be made to fit any space. It can be hung from hooks on the ceiling to divide a large space, or between rooms.

Materials

Ostrich feathers—taken from a feather duster
Colored tracing paper or other translucent paper—you need one letter sheet (8 1/2 x 11 in.) per panel
Scalpel and steel ruler
Spray glue
Laminating machine (try local copier shops)
Small metal eyelets—4 per panel; eyelet tool
Attractive metal hooks—two per panel
Small sailing fasteners to hang them up—two per top panel
Screw hooks for affixing—two per top panel

1   *Fold each sheet of tracing paper in half.*
2   *Cut off the bulky ends of the quills, then shave off any thickness further up on both sides. Take off the bottom few fronds if needed.*
3   *Try out a selection of feathers on the tracing paper to check the size and proportion.*
4   *Using the scalpel, trim the tracing paper to a better size to suit the feathers, but don't cut the fold.*
5   *Open out one piece of tracing paper and arrange the feather on one side. Position, then lift it off. Working in a well-ventilated area, spray a light film of glue over the inside of the tracing paper.*
6   *Position the feather. Don't move it, but you may be able to tweak the top fronds.*
7   *Lower the top part of the fold over the feather and smooth. Using the flat of your hand, smooth the tracing paper from the fold to the cut edges to exclude air bubbles. Firm up the crease.*
8   *Have the edges trimmed and the panels laminated at a copy shop.*
9   *Affix an eyelet in the corner of each panel and use the hooks to link them together.*
10 *Affix a fastener to the top eyelets and the screw eyes to the ceiling or archway.*

Index

Acknowledgments

Behind this book is a team of talents. Many thanks to the following:
To Jeanne Laine for her inspiration, unstinting support, for making up most of the curtain and blind projects with her own special touch, and for helping on all the photo sessions. To Richard Harrison Architects and Terry Harrison at Spacecraft for sharing their knowledge and access to their libraries and to Terrance Riley for the inspiration of his book Light construction, published by The Museum of Modern Art, New York. To Tino Tedaldi for his wonderful light-filled photographs that fill most of the pages; and to Tom Leighton and Simon Upton who also contributed in a special way. To Debbie Mole for designing the pages so exquisitely against all the odds. To Susan Berry, for having the vision to create a book on sheers in the first place. And finally to my wonderful family, Richard, Zoe and Faye for their support and patience throughout the hectic months during which I was creating the book.

My special thanks go to the following, who generously opened up their homes for photography for this book: Anna French, Marilyn Phipps and Josephine Ryan.

T=top, **C**=center, **B**=bottom, **L**=left, **R**=right.

PHOTOGRAPHIC CREDITS
10 Fritz von der Schulenberg/The Interior Archive; 11 Fritz von der Schulenberg/The Interior Archive; 12 L: Rodney Hyett/EWA; R: Rodney Hyett/EWA; 13 R: Henry Wilson/The Interior Archive (Designer: Denise Lee); 16 T: Edina van der Wyck/The Interior Archive (Designer: Atlanta Bartlett); B: Simon McBride/The Interior Archive (Owner: Nerida Piggia) 17 Simon McBride/The Interior Archive (Owner Nerida: Piggia) 20 T: Tim Beddow/The Interior Archive (Architect: Craig Hamilton) B: EWA; 21 T: Fritz von der Schulenberg (Architect Nico Rensch); B: Andrew Wood/Interior Archive (Owner: Jo Malone); 26 Simon Upton/C & B; 32 Simon Upton/C & B; 38/39 Simon Upton/C & B. 56–59: Simon Upton/C & B. 82 Fritz von der Schulenberg/The Interior Archive (Architect Nico Rensch); 84 EWA; 86 L: Tim Street-Porter/EWA; R: EWA; 90 L & R: Tom Leighton for Dulux Colour Magazine. Styling Tessa Evelegh; 92 L & R: Tom Leighton for Dulux Colour Magazine. Styling Tessa Evelegh; 94 L & R: Tom Leighton for Dulux Colour Magazine. Styling Tessa Evelegh.

PROPS CREDITS
6 Four-poster bed, side table and occasional table, Furniture in Style by Lena Proudlock. Bedlinen: The White Company; 26 Chair, Tobias and The Angel; 29 Curtain in Tapia Madras; 38 Anna French; 30 L: Tapia Madras; 38 Anna French; CT: Voile in 'Simple' designed by Laurence Llewlyn-Bowen for Graham & Brown; Centre CM: Voile in 'Little' designed by Laurence Llewlyn-Bowen for Graham & Brown; Centre CB: Voile in 'Sexy' designed by Laurence Llewlyn-Bowen for Graham & Brown; 32 Onion chair from Tobias and the Angel; 36 Bees voile V26, Anna French; 40 L: Green and white voile, Indus 03 from the Shahbash Collection, Malabar; C: Peachy voile, Tum Tum 02, from the Shahbash Collection, Malabar; R: Green and yellow voile with cord, Shahbash 02, from the Shahbash Collection, Malabar; 42 Nickel curtain pole with Knot finial, Artisan; 43 C: Stinson curtain jewellery Shell Droplets by Artisan; 44 B: Stinson curtain jewelry Clear Glass Droplets by Artisan; 55 TR: Sheer fabric with lotus applique, Takoradi 02 from the Shahbash Collection, Malabar; 62 Lattice Roller blind with earthenware bead pull by eclectics; 63 TR Natural colored wooden Venetian blind from eclectics mail-order. BR: Canvas reefed blind from eclectics mail order; 64 Cotton roller blinds in Burnt Orange, Midnight, and Apple from eclectics; 72 Antique chair, Josephine Ryan; 78 Translucent bead curtain, Idonia van der Bijl; 80 Antique gilded cupboard, Josephine Ryan; 83 C: Shelf unit on wheels, The Holding Company; 90 Paint: shutters and woodwork, 60YY 69/448, skirtings, 90YY72/323, both Satinwood. Walls, 90YY 72/323 Matt Emulsion, all from the Colour Palette range from the Dulux in-store mixing system. Shutters made to measure from Gooding Aluminium. Table and chairs, branches of Habitat; 92 Paint: Screens, 30BG 64/108, skirtings, 70BB 44/144, both Satinwood. Walls, 70BB 44/144 all from the Colour Palette range, from the Dulux in-store mixing system. Freestanding screens made to order by Jali. Bed, The Iron Bed Company. Bedlinen, The Laundry; 94 Paint: Reclaimed shutters painted with two coats of Limed Oak Woodwash from the Dulux Special Effects range. Walls, 90YR 48/062; 96 Screen made to order by Leonie Macdonald, 52a Alexandra Road, Weymouth, Dorset DT4 7QQ; email: leonie@mac52.freeserve.co.uk ; 98 Bead screen, Idonia van de Bijl; 104 Fabrics: Quentin Check Voile 74 and Edgar Voile 77, both Anna French; Polished steel curtain rail, clear glass Timo finials and Clear Glass Droplets, all Artisan; 106 four-poster bed, side table and occasional table, Furniture in Style by Lena Proudlock. Bedlinen: The White Company.